D0712281

Essays by Divers Hands

VOLUME XXXVIII

Essays by Divers Hands

BEING THE TRANSACTIONS OF THE
ROYAL SOCIETY OF LITERATURE

NEW SERIES · VOLUME XXXVIII

EDITED BY

JOHN GUEST, M.A., F.R.S.L.

LONDON
OXFORD UNIVERSITY PRESS
NEW YORK   TORONTO
1975

Oxford University Press, Ely House, London W. 1

GLASGOW NEW YORK TORONTO MELBOURNE WELLINGTON
CAPE TOWN IBADAN NAIROBI DAR ES SALAAM LUSAKA ADDIS ABABA
DELHI BOMBAY CALCUTTA MADRAS KARACHI LAHORE DACCA
KUALA LUMPUR SINGAPORE HONG KONG TOKYO

Printed in Great Britain
at the University Press, Oxford
by Vivian Ridler
Printer to the University

CONTENTS

INTRODUCTION

Essays by Divers Hands appears approximately every other year. Since, for reasons of size and cost, each volume contains only nine or ten contributions, not all the lectures delivered to the Society over the period can be included. But the Editor has less choice than might be supposed. The lectures which do not appear have not necessarily been rejected or overlooked. Many authors lecture from notes only, from headings—and the writing out and preparation for press of a seven-thousand-word talk is a job which some are disinclined to do. Again, certain lectures are specifically designed to be heard rather than read. Max Beerbohm, as we learn from Sir Harold Acton's delightfully entertaining essay in this volume, included a Prefatory Note to *Mainly on the Air*, a collection of his broadcast talks, in which he emphasized that the talks were composed for the ears of his listeners; in writing for the ear only, he did not 'express himself in just the way that would be his if he were writing for the eye as well. . . . I would therefore', he added, 'take the liberty of advising you to read these broadcasts aloud to yourself—or to ask some friend to read them aloud to you.' While not going so far as to suggest that Fellows and Members should press their friends and relations into reading the ensuing essays aloud to *them*, I would ask them to bear in mind what might perhaps these days be called 'the audio factor'. The essays which follow may not therefore, by some infallible editorial choice, be absolutely the best in every possible respect that were delivered to the Society since the last volume appeared—but how excellent they all are.

Looking back, as I have done recently, over the volumes of *Essays by Divers Hands* covering the last twenty or so years, one cannot but be impressed by the extraordinarily high level of the writing they contain, by the distinction of the contributors, and by the interest and variety of the subject-matter covered. This modest-looking series with its quaint title (hints of sub-aqueous activity—perhaps even fishing for pearls) really deserves to be better known. Each volume contains a panel of 'names' which any publisher could only dream of seeing brought together on his list. Nor, in spite of the august auspices under which the essays are produced, is there the slightest trace of solemnity about them. Seriousness there may be; that is another matter; but of the ten essays which follow, for instance, no less than six—at least, in places—are very funny indeed: Sir Harold Acton on Max Beerbohm is a delight; Brian Fothergill's dry asides on the extravagances of Beckford's life came through wonderfully in his delivery of the lecture, as they now do on paper; Montgomery Hyde on Henry James—perhaps especially on the Master ordering six two-pound pots of Oxford marmalade from the Army and Navy Stores—is unforgettable; Michael Holroyd, highly entertaining on the boisterous relationship between Wyndham Lewis and Augustus John; Giles St. Aubyn's essay on Queen Victoria as an author—a pure comic gem (I defy anyone to read it without laughing aloud); and finally, not without sadness, William Plomer's talk on Kilvert and his Diary from which Mrs. Dew's expedition by train to Hereford—as William Plomer himself read it—was a joy. This whole essay, indeed, induces a contented smile; and it is in the reading of this last piece that I can still very clearly hear the author's voice—that precise, kindly, unemphatic but authoritative voice which gave on so many occasions such pleasure to this Society and which, to our loss, we shall not hear again.

Of the remaining four essays, each is an important contribution to its subject. Ronald Blythe, winner of the Society's Heinemann Award with *Akenfield*, his richly detailed study of Suffolk village life, analyses in 'The Dangerous Idyll' the role of peasant writers and, indeed, the whole attitude of writers to the rural in literature. Dilys Powell comes to some surprising and illuminating conclusions in examining the sort of books that best lend themselves to being filmed. A. W. Raitt, in a scholarly and exceptionally elegant essay, discusses Flaubert's achievement as a short-story writer. And Constance Babington Smith, the biographer of Rose Macaulay, describes her work with particular reference to her love of language, of words in themselves. One is grateful for a bonus within this essay: a lengthy quoted passage from Rose Macaulay's *Personal Pleasures*, a rhapsody about words which, although a highly self-conscious, almost—one might say—a self-mocking, literary exercise, is such a stunning *tour de force* that the reader is tempted to applaud.

For all these contributions—published, and listened-to but maybe unpublished—for all the care taken in their preparation, and the pleasure given by their delivery, our thanks.

JOHN GUEST

KATJA REISSNER LECTURE

This lecture perpetuates the memory of Katja Reissner, musician and lover of literature, who died in December 1952. It was founded by her son, Alexander Reissner, a member of this Society since 1946.

MAX BEERBOHM: A DANDY AMONG ENGLISH CLASSICS

By SIR HAROLD ACTON, C.B.E., D.LITT., F.R.S.L.

(Read 15 November 1973)

Lord David Cecil, C.H., C.Lit., D.Litt., F.R.S.L., in the Chair

FINE writing is often thrust between inverted commas and regarded in a derogatory light by modern book reviewers as something decadent, decorative and ultimately futile. Apparently writing should be anything but fine, and the writer should avoid any hint of culture except in a disparaging tone of voice. Above all, he should avoid any literary flavour like the plague. 'Powerful' is perhaps the modern critic's most laudatory adjective, to which 'compelling' and 'compassionate' are often added; and any prose that is muddled, cluttered, obscure, obscene, and tiring to read, may pass muster as powerful and compelling, if not compassionate.

Max Beerbohm was consistently a fine writer within a narrow range—perhaps the last of his kind in the English language—and he was never ashamed of being literary. There is a passage in *Zuleika Dobson* where he smiles at this idiosyncrasy. The ducal hero inquires of Zuleika: 'You have never dipped into the Greek pastoral poets, nor sampled the Elizabethan sonneteers?'

'No, never. You will think me lamentably crude: my experience of life has been drawn from life itself.'

'Yet often you talk as though you had read rather much. Your way of speech has what is called "the literary flavour".'

'Ah, that is an unfortunate trick which I caught from a writer, a Mr. Beerbohm, who once sat next to me at dinner somewhere. I can't break myself of it. I assure you I hardly ever open a book. Of life, though, my experience has been very wide. . . .'

The special form of prose composition in which Max Beerbohm excelled, the essay, was, more than other forms, a gradual distillation of European culture since the Renaissance. Its pioneers were Montaigne in France and Bacon in England. With Addison, Steele, and Goldsmith in the eighteenth century the essay became established as a literary convention essentially polite and companionable. In the nineteenth century nearly every aspiring author tried his hand at it and, as Lord Birkenhead remarked, 'the whimsicalities of Lamb and his disciples were exploited beyond endurance'. The raw material of Lamb's essays was less important than the treatment, but his sweetness was converted to saccharine by his imitators. However, he imposed a style and set a fashion which lasted in England until the beginning of this century. It seemed easy and looked spontaneous, yet Lamb confessed that his lucid and apparently facile confidences were 'wrung from him with slow pain'. Most of his followers indulged in a sort of rambling sentimental prattle. It became quite remunerative: many turned out an essay a week for a modest livelihood. Aldous Huxley satirized the type in *Antic Hay*. Some of you may remember sleek Mr. Mercaptan, who 'had a style and used it, delightfully, in his middle articles for the literary weeklies. His most precious work, however, was that little volume of essays, prose poems, vignettes and paradoxes, in which he had so brilliantly illustrated his favourite theme— the pettiness, the simian limitations, the insignificance, and the absurd pretentiousness of *Homo* soi-distant *Sapiens*. Those who met Mr. Mercaptan personally often came away with the feeling that perhaps, after all, he was right in judging so severely of humanity.'

Those chatty middle articles have vanished together with the literary weeklies. Very few Victorian and Edwardian essayists succeed in riveting our attention today. Max Beerbohm was the great exception: he was their final, most exquisite flower. The scent is still fragrant—the flower has not withered, thanks to Lord David Cecil and a few who continue to water it.

Though Max died as late as 19 May 1956, he never ceased to be a figure of the eighteen-nineties. His first collection of essays, humorously entitled *The Works of Max Beerbohm*, was published in 1896. Already, at the age of twenty-four, his salient qualities are apparent in this slender volume. Several of these essays had appeared previously in the then notorious *Yellow Book* and had been swallowed with deadly earnestness and disapproval by Late Victorian reviewers. *Punch* lost whatever sense of humour it possessed and railed against *A defence of Cosmetics* in halting rhyme. The professional humorist Barry Pain described it as 'the very rankest and most nauseous thing in literature that I have ever read'. The critics thought, as Lord David Cecil wrote, that 'he was seriously attempting to undermine man's natural reverence for God's handiwork'. Of course Max had his tongue in his cheek half the time. He could not resist teasing the Victorian Pharisees as Evelyn Waugh and Nancy Mitford have teased the Marxist Puritans of today. He revelled in what he called his *succès de fiasco*, which enhanced his literary reputation. While his mischievous sense of fun was youthful and remained so, his manner and style were precociously mature. The main features of his character were formed at Oxford. In this respect Wilde's remark about him is true: 'The gods have bestowed on Max the gift of perpetual old age.'

The influence of Wilde and Pater on his early development was even greater than the influence of Latin and Greek. Pater he parodied and laughed at for treating English as a dead language, but he had absorbed the doctrine of Pater's *Renaissance*: he burned always 'with a hard gemlike flame' as Pater expressed it. The comedian and cartoonist was tinged with the aestheticism of the period, dominated by the dandyism of Oscar Wilde, who had told Max that his style was 'like a silver dagger'. His charming story *The Happy Hypocrite*, first published in 1896, owes much to *Dorian Gray* and Wilde's theory of the mask. According to this, we creatures of chaotic impulse should assume a mask representing our ideal of what we aspire to be.

The mask recurred frequently in Wilde's writings and conversation. 'Man is least himself when he talks in his own person. Give him a mask and he will tell you the truth.' Lord George Hell, the profligate hero of *The Happy Hypocrite*, falls in love with the demure young dancer Jenny Mere, who tells him in a speech very redolent of Wilde: 'I can never be the wife of any man whose face is not saintly. Your face, my lord, mirrors, it may be, true love for me, but it is even as a mirror long tarnished by the reflection of this world's vanity. It is even as a tarnished mirror. Do not kneel to me, for I am poor and humble. I was not made for such impetuous wooing. Kneel, if you please, to some greater, gayer lady. As for my love, it is my own, nor can it ever be torn from me, but given, as true love needs be given, freely. Ah rise from your knees. That man, whose face is wonderful as the faces of the saints, to him I will give my true love.'

Lord George Hell procures the mask of a saint from Mr. Aeneas, the fashionable mask-maker, and he is subsequently transformed—so that when the mask is torn from his face by one of his former mistresses, 'Line for line, feature for feature, it was the same. 'Twas a saint's face.' The parallel with *Dorian Gray* is evident.

In his youth at any rate Max appeared to believe in Wilde's dictum: 'The future belongs to the dandy. It is the exquisites who are going to rule.' He remained a dandy and an exquisite all his life, wilfully isolating himself in semi-retirement from a world where dandies were gradually demoted to Beatles and the exquisites were crushed or silenced by technology.

Only two years before his death Somerset Maughan, who was to survive him, remarked to Garson Kanin, discussing the passage of time and its effect on authors: 'Max solved the problem of outgrowing his time by stepping out of it. What he did was to leave London, leave England, and move to Rapallo, where he continues to live as if he were still living at the turn of the century. He dresses in the same way, reads pretty much what he read then, writes practically nothing, nor does he draw. He has frozen himself, as it were, in time. But what's most astonishing is that without lifting a finger he becomes more and more famous, more celebrated and highly thought of. Someone said that his reputation grows with every book he doesn't write. Whereas I keep working like a bloody fool and am constantly told that it's not as good as my last.'

Another lesson Max learned from Master Wilde was to respect his own limitations. 'It has often been made a subject of reproach against artists and men of letters that they are lacking in wholeness and completeness of nature. As a rule this must necessarily be so. That very concentration of vision and inversity of purpose which is the characteristic of the artistic temperament is in itself a mode of limitation. To those who are preoccupied with the beauty of form nothing else seems of so much importance.'

When he was rising fifty, Max explained to Bohun Lynch who proposed to write a book about him: 'My gifts are small. I've used them very well and discreetly, never straining them;

and the result is that I've made a charming little reputation.'
He had never strained his gifts but he had continued to polish
and perfect them, looking backward rather than forward into
the future. As he wrote of Beau Brummell in his early essay on
Dandies: 'He was ever most economical, most scrupulous of
means. Treatment was everything to him.'

The famous figures of his halcyon youth continued to haunt
him half a century later with a nostalgic aura of glamour.
Here I cannot deal specifically with his caricatures which must
be seen to be appreciated, for many of these were literary
criticisms and footnotes to history made visible. Those in *The
Poet's Corner*, for instance, extremely funny in their irreverence,
engrave certain scenes on the memory which rise mischievously
before one's eyes when one peruses the poet in question.
Who can forget 'Mr. Tennyson, reading *In Memoriam* to his
Sovereign'—the vast abstemiously furnished room, with the
Prince Consort framed above the chimneypiece, the lion and
unicorn clock, the empty fire grate, the prim pattern on walls
and carpet, and the dumpy Widow of Windsor with her toes on
a red footstool, listening to the bearded bard? Or the florid-
faced 'Robert Browning taking tea with the Browning Society'—
a dreary group of his dowdy devotees? The *Rossetti and his Circle*
series which he produced later are like a critical biography of
the poet and his Pre-Raphaelite brethren. A self-caricature
drawn in 1893 was no doubt a good resemblance, but it was
also the pattern of the wistful dandy Max wished to appear,
'stiff-necked, over-hatted, wasp-waisted,' as he wrote of the
Regency dandies—'in fact, the very deuce of a pose'. The pose,
which infuriated those 'who called a spade a spade', was most
transparent in *The Works*, where he introduced French words
like rococo curls and coined quaint expressions like 'pop-limbo'
and 'trip the cockawhoop' and Latinisms à la Pater. His
paradoxes were Oscarian: 'Childhood has always seemed to me
the tragic period of life. To be subject to the most odious
espionage at the one age when you never dream of doing
wrong, to be deceived by your parents, thwarted of your
smallest wish, oppressed by the terrors of manhood and of the
world to come, and to believe, as you are told, that childhood
is the only happiness known: all this is quite terrible.'

These early essays are more mannered than the later ones,
and their vocabulary is consciously absurd, but they are the
leisurely creations of a fastidious mind. The deceptively casual
caricaturist becomes a Persian miniaturist in prose. His

humorously affectionate evocation of George IV has imposed itself on a generation which came round to admire the Brighton Pavilion and the Banqueting Room at Windsor. *The Pervasion of Rouge* was prophetic for all its ebullient coxcombry. And the fanciful picture of his premature retirement from the world after leaving Oxford in *Diminuendo* was also prophetic of his ultimate retirement to Rapallo. In mock disillusion since meeting Pater during his first year at Oxford he resolved to avoid 'sensations', 'pulsations', and 'exquisite moments' that were not purely intellectual. 'I would make myself master oi some small area of physical life, a life of quiet, monotonous simplicity, exempt from all outer disturbance, I would shield my body from the world that my mind might range over it, not hurt nor fettered.'

The last paragraph of *Diminuendo*, in which he feigns a premature fatigue, has often been quoted: 'Already I feel myself to be a trifle outmoded. I belong to the Beardsley period. Younger men, with months of activity before them, with fresher schemes and notions, with newer enthusiasm, have pressed forward since then. *Cedo junioribus.* Indeed, I stand aside with no regret. For to be outmoded is to be a classic, if one has written well. I have acceded to the hierarchy of good scribes and rather like my niche.'

That was written in 1895. Even then Max was toying with an idea which was to become a reality. Very consciously he continued to belong to 'the Beardsley period' and to remain a classic well satisfied with his niche. He had no false modesty about his achievements, and he never wrote down to an ill-educated public.

More followed *The Works* after a leisurely interval, in 1899. This contained his warm appreciation of the ridiculed and depreciated Ouida, and was gracefully dedicated to 'Mlle de la Ramée with the author's compliments and to Ouida with his love.' Here he confesses: 'For my part, I am a dilettante, a *petit maître*. I love best in literature delicate and elaborate ingenuities of form and style. But my preference does not keep me from paying homage to Titanic force, and delighting, now and again, in its manifestation." He goes on to praise the sustained vitality of Ouida's writings, such a contrast with his own: 'Her every page is a riot of unpolished epigrams and unpolished poetry of vision, with a hundred discursions and redundancies. . . . Her style is a veritable cascade.'

In this illuminating essay Max also refers admiringly to the plethoric abundance of Meredith's ideas and to the stunning exuberance of Swinburne's rhapsodies. To Swinburne he returned later, and one of his most poignant essays—I hesitate to call it perfect amid so much perfection—'No. 2. The Pines', evokes his meeting with the poet when he was old and deaf and jealously guarded by Watts-Dunton. His admiration for Swinburne lasted until his death, shortly before which he murmured a stanza from *The Garden of Proserpine*—

> From too much love of living,
> From hope and fear set free,
> We thank with brief thanksgiving
> Whatever gods may be
> That no life lives for ever;
> That dead men rise up never;
> That even the weariest river
> Winds somewhere safe to sea.

Max was still under thirty when *More* was published. In 1898 he succeeded Bernard Shaw as drama critic for the *Saturday Review* (then under the lively editorship of Frank Harris), a position he held reluctantly till 1910, when he married Florence Kahn, a shy American actress—Ada Leverson remarked of her that she had left the stage before anybody knew she had been on it—and left London for Rapallo. The youngest of a large family of German-Balt origin, Max had lived at home with his mother until he married a second mother as it were.

In 1898 he also began to write *Zuleika Dobson*, which he did not finish until 1911. This, as Lord David Cecil stated in his biography, is 'the most ambitious of all his literary works, the most elaborate and highly wrought in style and his only full-length story, it also represents his art at its most quintessential: in it his distinguishing characteristics appear in their most extreme form'. E. M. Forster has remarked penetratingly that it has 'a beauty unattainable by serious literature . . . it is so funny and charming, so iridescent, yet so profound'.

With all these virtues, and in spite of the magical evocation of the Oxford of Max's undergraduate period, it is the only one of Max's writings in which I feel a slight sense of strain—that the joke is carried too far. Yet the blend of fantasy and fact in this tale of communal suicide for the sake of the ruthless Zuleika is certainly unique, a *tour de force* of indiluted artistry. Some of the details and digressions may detract from the flow of the narrative, yet when we pick up the book they still exert an enduring fascination.

As he wrote to his friend Reggie Turner, Max did not expect *Zuleika Dobson* to be anything like a popular success, but he did think it had a chance of surviving 'as a treasure for experts in fine literature, and especially for such of those experts as are or have been or shall have been Oxford men'. The book, he said correctly, 'has its quality, invulnerable'. It was a labour of nostalgic love for Oxford whose physical presence permeates it as much as Capri does *South Wind*. He chiselled and polished the pages like precious stones during the twelve years he contributed his weekly articles on the theatre to the *Saturday Review*.

Recently I attempted to read Mr. Norman Mailer's biography of Marilyn Monroe, whom he had never met but often dreamed about. 'I'm probably one of the better fast writers in the world now', Mr. Mailer asserted. He wrote this book in frantic haste and 285,000 copies of it were printed immediately. The critics described it as 'compulsively readable' but I was not compelled. I turned to *Zuleika Dobson* with renewed delight. Remote as they are in time and place, both heroines are unquestionably feminine—equally hard and bright. But there the analogy fades. Max has portrayed the type once for all with the right admixture of irony and frivolity.

In an article entitled 'Why I ought not to have become a dramatic critic', he coolly asserted: 'I am not fond of the theatre. Dramatic art interests and moves me less than any of the other arts . . . I confess that I have never regarded any theatre as much more than the conclusion to a dinner or the prelude to a supper'—summing up with: 'I daresay there are many callings more uncomfortable and dispiriting than that of dramatic critic. To be a porter on the Underground Railway must, I have often thought, be very terrible. Whenever I feel myself sinking under the stress of my labours, I shall say to myself, 'I am not a porter on the Underground Railway.'

Looking back to his twelve years as dramatic critic, he admitted that he had acquired a vivid interest in the theatre though the writing of those weekly articles had always been a burden and he felt extraordinarily light and gay in bidding his readers farewell. He agreed with Charles Lamb about the toil of literary composition. 'Writing has always been uphill work to me, mainly because I am cursed with an acute literary conscience. To seem to write with ease and delight is one of the duties which a writer owes to his readers, his art. And to contrive that effect involves very great skill and care: it is a matter of technique, a matter of construction partly, and partly of choice of words and cadences.'

Max's collected articles from the *Saturday Review*, entitled *Around Theatres*, illustrate his preferences and prejudices so wittily and urbanely that one can read them for pleasure today, long after the plays and actors he criticizes have passed into oblivion. Substitute a few names here and there, and much of his criticism applies to modern plays and actors, but he is more honest than most of our critics. He damns—but never with faint praise.

Because these articles deal with so much dead wood, as it were, those who are not regular Maximilians might not be tempted to read them, which would be their loss. The spur of those dreaded Thursdays (the days chosen by him, as being the last possible, for writing his articles) forced him to write with a greater speed and spontaneity. Some plays he slates unmercifully, but he is positively exhilarating on such occasions. Perhaps his most devastating is the critique of Jerome K. Jerome's long-forgotten drama *The Passing of the Third Floor Back* which enjoyed a popular success in its day, largely owing to Forbes-Robertson's fine performance in it.

Entitled 'A Deplorable Affair', this begins: 'In the course of a theatrical season, the critic's proud spirit is gradually subdued. Twaddling play succeeds twaddling play and, as the wearisome procession goes by, the critic's protests become fainter: he begins to acquiesce in what cannot, apparently, be stopped. But when he comes back after a holiday, with a fresh eye, with a soul invigorated by contact with real things and lovely things and things that matter, and comes just in time to see the same old procession starting placidly forth on the same old route, then, oh then, it needs a very great effort in him to control his temper. Why should he try? I shall *not* try. All for art, and the temper well lost, I say.' And in view of the play's evident success he exclaims: 'What can be hoped of an art which must necessarily depend on the favour of the public—of such a public, at least, as ours? Good work may, does sometimes, succeed. But never with the degree of success that befalls twaddle and vulgarity unrelieved. Twaddle and vulgarity will have always the upper hand.'

This was written in 1908, and it seems to me to be as true now as it was then, though the twaddle and vulgarity in vogue today happen to be more pretentious, overlaid with a pseudo-intellectual veneer.

Around Theatres contains many gems which still shine brightly through the mist of half a century. Among these I should select 'An Adramatist'—a critique of *The Grey Stocking* by Maurice Baring, which is as amusingly incisive as Max's best caricatures. But each of Max's essays should be read in its entirety. When a lady wrote asking him if she might extract some paragraphs from an essay to be included in an anthology, he explained to her: 'My essays have many faults, but they have the virtue of being very closely written. Every paragraph in any of them depends on every other paragraph; and every sentence on every other sentence. That is what gives them the modest quality of *life*, of *movement*. A dead bird can be carved acceptably: a bit of breast, a leg, a liver—wing, and so on. But oh, don't mutilate a live bird. Let it fly, let it sing. Don't chop off bits of it. Don't hand such bits round. They aren't good to eat.'

Crime, sociology, political commitment, and the depression of audiences appear to be the chief concerns of the modern playwright with an omnipotent State theatre in view as his ideal. To its adepts an aesthete of Max's calibre must be anathema, since he was in favour of artistic unity and intelligent entertainment. I rather doubt if he would applaud that 'mastery of the savage interchange of domestic small talk' displayed in *Who's Afraid of Virginia Woolf?* and other recent hits. I suspect he would say, as of Gorky's *The Lower Depths*, that this was 'no slice of life. It is chunks, hunks, shreds and gobbets, clawed off anyhow, chucked at us anyhow. . . . Mere gall is no better than mere sugar. It is worse.'

But I must not stray from my theme—those essays in which his talent achieved supremacy. I concur with Evelyn Waugh that he was less happy in pure narration, though exceptions should be made for 'Enoch Soames' and 'Maltby and Braxton' in *Seven Men*; 'Savonarola Brown' should be placed among his parodies. One must be familiar with the authors he parodied to appreciate the full brilliance of *A Christmas Garland*, published in 1912. Henry James called the book 'the most intelligent that has been produced in England for many a long day'. Lord David Cecil relates that an admirer asked Henry James his opinion on some question. 'Ask that young man,' he said, pointing to Max who was at the same party, 'he is in full possession of my innermost thoughts.'

And Even Now, published in 1920, contains Max's ripest essays, the cream of his cream. Some English writers, as he said, were weight-lifters, others jugglers with golden balls. He never attempted to join the weight-lifters; often he juggled with golden balls whose glittering evolutions dazzle the reader-spectator.

'No. 2. The Pines', 'Hosts and Guests', 'A Clergyman', each of these is perfect in its way. Nobody else could have produced them. 'A Relic' evokes a naïf young man's first effort to write a story 'in the manner of great Guy de Maupassant' after witnessing a scene on the terrace of a casino in Normandy between a short fat man and a younger woman who smashes a fan in a fit of ill temper, the stump of which is the relic. The aspirant author never gets beyond the sentence, 'Down below, the sea rustled to and fro over the shingle.' ('These words, which pleased me much, were to do double duty. They were to recur. They were to be, by a fine stroke, the very last words of my tale, their tranquillity striking a sharp ironic contrast with the stress of what had just been narrated.')

'How shall I word it?' incorporates some refreshingly abusive imaginary letters—'from Poor Man to obtain Money from Rich One', 'from Young Man refusing to pay his Tailor's Bill', 'to thank Author for Inscribed Copy of Book', etc. (My own preferences are those 'from Young Lady in Answer to Invitation from Old Schoolmistress' and 'in acknowledgement of Wedding Present'.)

As we read on, the golden balls melt into a golden sunset—what Max might describe as 'flammiferous'— a sunset rather than a sunrise, for Max dwells with more relish on his past than on his present, and on the novelists and statesmen of the past. Among his cartoons, for instance, there is one entitled 'English Fiction—Ancient and Modern':

i. Ancient. The hero trying to control a guilty passion. (Quite dramatic and interesting, this.)

ii. Modern. The Hero trying to muster up a guilty passion. (Less dramatic, surely, and less interesting.)

And another entitled 'Parerga of Statesmanship':

Statesman of the Olden Time, making without wish for emolument a flat but faithful version of the Georgics, in English hexameters.

Statesman of Today, doing one of the articles in his powerful series, 'Men I've Been Up Against,' for the *Sunday Rumpus*. (Terms, £75 a line. Grammar and style touched up in the Office.)

Externally the private life of Max Beerbohm was uneventful. Though much sought after by London hostesses as a witty talker who was also a charming person, he retired, as I have mentioned, to Rapallo with his shy bride in 1910, and there he remained (except during part of the First World War and during the last one) until he died forty-six years later, content with his modest means, his small circle of devoted friends, and his consummate craftsmanship. 'I have a public of 1,500', he remarked at the height of his fame.

Rapallo gave him the peace of mind, the requisite distance from the madding crowd, the protection from that Industrial System which he had to accept with a shudder of distaste. One of his drawings is entitled 'Civilisation and the Industrial System'. A personification of the latter says 'No, my dear, you may've ceased to love me; but you took me for better or wuss in younger and 'appier days, and there'll be no getting away for you from me, ever.'

Relatively impecunious as he was, Max did succeed in getting away. Rapallo was much quieter in 1910 than it is now, and his little house on the road to Zoagli, 'about twenty-five minutes walk *up*, and twenty *down*', fulfilled his material requirements. From the Villino Chiaro he wrote to his old friend Reggie Turner: 'It is no news merely to say that I am consciously happy during sixteen hours of the daily twenty-four, and unconsciously happy during the other eight; and yet that is the only news I have. What goes to constitute that happiness would make a poor recital. Absolutely nothing 'happens'. Florence and I 'see' nobody: there is no one to see—except a good many German tourists who all look exactly alike. There are Italian peasants and tradesmen, to whom I say '*Buon Giorno*' with a singularly pure accent; but I haven't conversed with a single human being except Florence since we left England. . . . The sun shines, and the sea shines under it, and I eat a good deal twice a day, and the camellias are just beginning to bloom, and the oranges and lemons are ripe, and I do a great deal of work, and everything goes on from day to day with a heavenly sameness of peace and happiness.' (15 Nov. 1910).

'The great deal of work' included his cartoons, over which he took a great deal of trouble, deriving a sensuous pleasure from the process of colouring them. But he also spent much time 'improving', as he called it, the title-pages and illustrations of various books in his library. These 'improvements' involved grotesque alterations of the features, adding bulbous noses and squinting eyes, as well as absurd press notices and fancy dedications in forged handwriting. He had great fun with Queen Victoria's 'More Leaves from the Journal of a Life in the Highlands'. He also produced wooden dummies of books with such titles as 'The Love Poems of Herbert Spencer', and decorated his villino with frescoes of Henry James and his other cherished models. He drew more and he wrote less, but he enjoyed himself like a child, chuckling over his own contrivances.

Few of his essays referred to Italy, yet it was his long residence there which had helped him to 'freeze himself in time', as Maugham expressed it. *A Stranger in Venice* appeared in 1906 and was all the finer for not being overladen with glib erudition. He may confuse Gentile with Giovanni Bellini, but how much clearer and lighter is this delicate pastel than the fussy oil paintings of the great majority! He captures the atmosphere seemingly without effort. Evelyn Waugh considered this to be 'the best travel-sketch ever written'. It is surely a work of art.

Having settled so happily at Rapallo, he was not tempted to travel. Towards the end of his life he was induced to broadcast, and his broadcasts delighted a wider public. Six of these were published in *Mainly on the Air* (1946). He had lost none of his fastidiousness. In a prefatory note of apology he emphasized that they were composed for the ears of listeners and that in writing for the ear only, he did not 'express himself in just the way that would be his if he were writing for the eye as well'. 'I would therefore,' he adds, 'take the liberty of advising you to read these broadcasts aloud to yourself—or to ask some friend to read them aloud to you.'

When the B.B.C. presented him with records of these talks he played them again and again, appreciating the mellow inflexions of his voice, revelling in the memories of the distant past they evoked. In 1937 he had written to Reggie Turner that he had been re-reading *Daisy Miller*, with 'pangs of longing for the dear delicate un-panic-stricken world of sixty years ago'. His greatest friend died in Florence in 1938, and perhaps Max's essay 'Laughter' is his best memorial.

In 1939 Max was knighted, not long before the outbreak of the Second World War. In youth he had scoffed at knighthood as 'a cheap commodity' scattered broadcast, while admitting 'there are few whose hands would not gladly grasp the dingy patent'. In old age the patent seemed less dingy. Persuaded by his wife, I imagine, he was glad to grasp it. Lady Beerbohm died in 1951, but he was fortunate in finding another companion, Miss Elisabeth Jungmann, to look after him in the winter of his old age. To assure her title to his modest estate he asked her to marry him when he was told he had little chance to recover from his last illness, and the Mayor of Rapallo performed the ceremony in the clinic where he lay. But I will spare you the last moments of the dying dandy who gallantly tried to be cheerful even then. Like most of us he would prefer to be remembered as he was while basking in the sunlight of his protracted prime.

THE DANGEROUS IDYLL: SWEET AUBURN TO AKENFIELD

By RONALD BLYTHE, F.R.S.L.

(Read 11 November 1971)

Michael Holroyd, F.R.S.L. in the Chair

IT may strike you as extraordinary—extreme—when I tell you
that any literary undertaking by an English villager, has until
quite recently, by which I mean the late nineteenth century,
been received with much the same suspicion as novels and
poetry written by English women. Each, by daring to produce
literature, had broken through ancient orderly concepts of their
functions. So at best they were odd and ingenious, and at worst
unnatural. John Clare didn't object to being called a peasant
and was great enough not to demand that he should always be
referred to as a poet. What helped to cripple him was the term
'peasant-poet', with its freakish implications. But this is what
he was called and the terrible conflict between his 'condition'
and his genius raged until it exploded into that vast, silencing
affirmation, I AM. Twice he made this huge nameless statement, perhaps in imitation of the profound claim he had heard
Yahveh make during the First Lesson in the village church,
though each time there was never a hint of pride or blasphemy.
Just the fact of John Clare. The first I AM poem is such a
perfect expression of a man's discovery of himself as superfluous,
unneeded and abandoned, that it speaks for every ignored man.
The second I AM poem, a sonnet, is different. It is Clare's
apology for being a poet:

> I feel I am, I only know I am
> And plod upon the earth as dull and void,
> Earth's prison chilled my body with its dram
> Of dullness, and my soaring thoughts destroyed.
> I fled to solitudes from passion's dream
> But strife pursued—I only know I am.
> I was a being created in the race
> Of men disdaining bounds of place and time—
> A spirit that could travel o'er the space
> Of earth and heaven—like a thought sublime,

Tracing creation, like my maker, free—
A soul unshackled like eternity,
Spurning earth's vain and soul debasing thrall
But now I only know I am—that's all.

What is a man's identity? Of what does it actually consist? That self which only he can feel and see? Or the conglomerant of job, address, appearance, class, and inherited name by which society recognizes him? How many a man, harnessed for life to what Geoffrey Grigson once called 'the penal labour of farm work', must have told himself I AM during the eighteenth and nineteenth centuries. And where such trapped lives were concerned, the nineteenth century ended during the 1940s.

In this talk I shall be mostly concerned with those who broke the harmonious rules of rural England by freeing themselves from such permissible literary expressions as ballads, folk-songs, saws and tales, eloquent and genuine though such things can be, and, by accepting themselves as very special 'beings created in the race of men', soared far beyond the words and music popularly associated with the fields. I shall also try to show how the great classic vision of the English countryside which the Augustans created, and which writers such as Clare, Bloomfield, Hardy and Burns challenged, which John Constable celebrated and which Jane Austen satirized, is not at all the same country vision which more and more occupies the conservationists of our own day.

The face of England, as thousands of sunny modern guide-books like to describe it, has remained wonderfully serene and unmarked in spite of the polluters. Neither its contemporary environmental problems nor its past tragedies—the Industrial Revolution, Micheldever, Tolpuddle, the clearances and enclosures, the squalid cottages which it upset John Constable to enter, the signs of greed and pride in the park—have marked it in such a way that its central beauty and inspiration have been defaced. In fact, we are at the beginning of a new cycle of reverence towards the countryside and its far from simple conditions. These we intuitively recognize as the result of a practical compromise made between the claims of neo-classical pastorals and intensive farming. The result of this combination has never been a particularly happy one for the ordinary countryman. It has had a way of limiting him in the eyes of the sophisticated, who see him as admirable but quaint. Quaintness was one of the things which Clare rejected when he cried, 'I am!' His father could sing ballads by the fireside and not make those who heard him feel uncomfortable. But when Clare read his first poems to his parents, or to the neighbours, he pretended that they were by someone else—an educated person—so that they did not have to feel that they were living with a kind of monster. And people still like village folk to 'fit', to stand upright and reassuring in the little innocent niches sentiment has carved out for them. They like to imagine village life as one of lasting and unchanging verities. To view it intellectually is thought vaguely treacherous.

Clare, when writing his autobiography, says that he was born in 'a gloomy village in Northamptonshire'. Gloomy or not, the sight of a single violet on Primrose Hill in London once caused him to hurry home to it. The incident illustrates the key factor in village experience: the fatal involvement, the need to remain. Robert Bloomfield wrote his enormously successful *The Farmer's Boy*—20,000 copies published—while he was working as a shoemaker in London. The poem was an act of nostalgia, for himself and for all his readers. Its appalling effect was to cut him off from his own village involvement for ever.

John Clare did the harder thing. He stayed in 'gloomy' Helpstone although from childhood on his isolation was to be intense. 'I live here among the ignorant like a lost man.' Charles Lamb advised him in his kindly fashion to do what all sensible poets did and 'transport Arcadia to Helpstone'. It was civilized advice inasmuch as it made clear to Clare that Lamb, by suggesting that the young ploughman was quite capable of using classical allusions and imagery, did not think of him as a peasant-poet. Yet Lamb had not understood. 'Gloomy' Helpstone—how the ecstatic nature poems refute the adjective!—*was* Arcady where Clare was concerned. When they forced him to live in a cottage only three miles away from this village which was part of him, he became mentally ill. And when they carried him to Northampton Asylum he eventually had to find a new persona to inhabit and chose, among others, Lord Byron's.

'That is where learning gets you!' his old mother believed. She thought learning 'the blackest arts of witchcraft' and Helpstone itself thought reading was synonymous with sloth. From about twelve years onward, Clare lived a furtive, aberrant existence, hiding in woods with his books, hoarding old sugar-bags to write on, muttering behind the plough. The village verses which, a century later, collectors like Cecil Sharp and Sabine Baring-Gould were to rescue from oblivion for the English Folk-Song Society, were, for Clare, so much trash. For him they merely reflected the ignorance from which he was determined to escape.

When he was thirteen, a young weaver showed him a scrap of Thomson's *The Seasons*. Now, if ever there was a single poem which moulded, sensitized, sentimentalized, elevated, and generally formed the British character during the eighteenth century it was *The Seasons*. It has been credited with being one of the chief agents to bring a spirit of tenderness and humanity to brutal Georgian England. For all that, the young weaver had no time for it because he was a Methodist. But he showed the scrap of it he possessed to this strange boy, who read these four lines, and was saved. Or lost. It all depends upon the value one places upon restless spiritual inquiry at the cost of content-ment. These are the four lines:

> Come gentle Spring, etherial mildness come
> And from the bosom of yon dropping cloud,
> While music wakes around, veil'd in a shower
> Of shadowing roses on our plains descend . . .

It isn't much, is it? And it is even less when we recall several hundred lines like it. But the fact is that for the path-seeking Clare the fragment hung in the workaday air of Helpstone, changing everything. His experience had something in common with that of James Northcote, the artist, who told Hazlitt that he had been life-long affected by an actor singing Shakespeare's 'Come unto these yellow sands, and then take hands', and that he felt it to be a kind of weakness or folly on his part. Hazlitt's reply was, 'There is no danger of that sort—all the real taste and feeling in the world is made up of what people take in their heads in this manner.'

There was precious little taste or feeling connected with what next happened at Helpstone. Unable to find time or even sufficient smoothed-out sugar-bags to establish the stream of poetry which Thomson's four lines had set flowing, Clare began what he called his 'muttering'. In other words, he spoke his poems softly into the Northamptonshire air, repeating the words many times until they no longer disappeared on the wind, but remained with him as whole and recognizable acts of creation. It was about this period, 1812, that poor Robert Bloomfield was reversing this process. His descent from the unsettling fame which the best-selling *Farmer's Boy* had brought him now included an attempt to make money by selling Aeolian harps.

So, while he heard that Murray the publisher had given 'Parson Crabbe £3000 for his Tales', Bloomfield had nothing more to offer *his* readers but simple home-made instruments to whine wordlessly in a gale. There is no evidence that they sold. And so we have this curious pen-less moment in the lives of the two poets, the once lionized Bloomfield hawking his wind-harps and the still unknown Clare entrusting the Northampton-shire air with his poetry because there was no other place for it.

As you can imagine, Helpstone did not take kindly to this muttering boy. Nor did the Marquess of Exeter's Master of the Kitchen Garden, who employed him. The persecution proper began at this point. So superb a creature had the master gardener seemed to Clare that, when applying for a job, he had sunk on his knees before him. The mockery being more than he could stand, he fled to the open fields. The fields to any village are its sea. The rancour and glances, the creeds and criticisms of the village centre, cannot be contained there. Solitude and the elemental processes of the growing year take over. People were always suggesting that the more refined task of gardening would suit such a delicate person but Clare found, throughout his working life, that labouring in a great field provided the best conditions for his happiness and his art. Eventually, it was his inability to do this work, as much as anything else, which hurried him towards madness.

Poets like Shelley might attempt to rouse his rural workers with,

> Men of England, wherefore plough
> —For the lords who lay ye low?
> The seed ye sow, another reaps,
> The wealth ye find, another keeps . . .

but John Clare, England's most articulate village voice, remained untouched by such revolutionary ideas. He ploughed in order to perfect what he called his 'descriptive rhyming'. Each night he wrote these spoken poems down and each day some of them vanished, as though mice had got hold of them—though it was only his mother stealing them 'for her own use as occasion called for them'. She thought he was only practising pothooks. But the realization that the ploughboy was up to something, with his mutterings and hidings, his starings at flowers and his traipsing after books to Stamford, soon leaked out, and the laughing began. When we read Clare's frequent references to it we at once appreciate that this was no ordinary touchiness but a flinching from what George Herbert once described as 'the mockery of murderers'.

The unnaturalness of Clare offended like the unnaturalness of writers such as Lady Winchilsea, the Duchess of Newcastle, Currer, Ellis and Acton Bell, and George Eliot when they claimed the same author's rights as men. In fact, when Lady Winchilsea scathingly attacked the system which allowed only males access to full literary expression, her words are curiously relevant to writers such as Clare whose 'condition' barred them from normal consideration as artists.

> How are we fallen! [she wrote]
> Fallen by mistaken rules,
> And Education's more than Nature's fools;
> Debarred from all improvements of the mind,
> And to be dull, expected and resigned;
> And if someone would soar above the rest,
> With warmer fancy, and ambition pressed,
> So strong the opposing faction still appears,
> The hopes to thrive can ne'er outweigh the fears.

Nothing finally outweighed the fears of Clare, as we know. We also know that he routed the picturesque pastoral and returned the landscape to its natural contours in the English imagination. The most overwhelming thing in his life was the revelation that he was no versifying rustic but a total poet. This knowledge was both terrible and wonderful. And Helpstone's laughter was probably generated as much by fear as by amusement.

For most of the eighteenth century a policy of moral and aesthetic containment had concealed a good deal of the pressures which were drastically altering the lives of the village people, still at this period the nation's largest labouring force. Because this containment was not imposed entirely from the top but possessed many deep cultural and religious elements springing from the people themselves, there were periods of classic harmony which, particularly during the famine which followed Napoleon's defeat in 1815, were looked back on by all classes as the golden years. Lord Ernle in his *History* says that the 1750s were the Golden Age of English agriculture. This euphoric memory seems to have resulted from the elegant propaganda disseminated by various painters, poets, landscape-gardeners and architects during the golden age itself, for in 1769 we have Oliver Goldsmith sending his new poem *The Deserted Village* to Sir Joshua Reynolds with the following letter attached:

How far you may be pleased with the versification and mere mechanical parts of this attempt, I do not pretend to enquire: but I *know* you will object (and indeed several of our best and wisest friends concur in the opinion) that the depopulation it deplores is *no where to be seen,* and the disorders it laments are only to be found in the poet's imagination. To this I can scarce make any other answer, than that I sincerely believe what I have written, that I have taken all possible pains in country excursions for these past four or five years to be certain of what I allege, and that all my views and enquiries have led me to believe those miseries real. . . . In regretting the depopulation of the countryside, I inveigh against the increase of our luxuries, and here also I expect the shout of modern politicians against me.

What had happened, of course, was that the unsightly inhabitants of Auburn had been tidied away to make a park. They had been resettled, as a matter of fact, though this was not the point. Like many a native in our own day, their ancestral homes and fields had to make way for 'civilization'. *The Deserted Village* remains a lasting indictment of white Africans at any time and in any place. For generations, on the principle that it couldn't happen here, the English liked to believe that Goldsmith's 'country excursions' must have taken place in his native Ireland, where things were different. But, as we know, Sweet Auburn was Nuneham Courtenay, Oxfordshire. And what Goldsmith was witnessing was a scene which, for a very different reason than the beautifying of a peer's new house, was soon to be familiar all over Britain. For the cruel if logical process by which the small independent farming units created by the manorial system were rationalized by 'enclosure' was soon to affect the country people. The enclosure of Helpstone runs as a disturbing counterpoint to the lyricism of Clare's poetry. Few villagers, however, were to describe these profound changes for, as Crabbe said,

> Few, amid the rural tribe, have time
> To number syllables, and play with rhyme.

George Crabbe, however, was the exception to every statement made about the peasant-poet for, having been born into the labouring classes and having heard, seen and experienced all their emotions, he totally and absolutely severed the connection when he became an established writer. The impetus behind his verse-tales is neither nostalgia nor enlightenment but a fastidious disenchantment with provincial life. He gazed at the individuals in the harsh little Suffolk community which he had abandoned with much the same dissecting accuracy as when his eye searched out the minute flora of the bitter shingle beach and the lonely marsh, except that he was apt to save his lyricism for the latter. He made no bones about his 'having fled from those shores'. 'Few men who have succeeded in breaking through the obscurity of their birth have retained so little trace of their origin', remarked one of his critics. Crabbe certainly made no bones about presenting his grimly brilliant anti-idyll in the same poetic form, the heroic couplet, in which Pope and other eighteenth-century writers had manufactured the idyll itself. These rhymed novels were packed with the sights and sounds which one was not supposed to see or hear on an excursion to the coast or to the fields. Worst of all, Crabbe had the audacity to examine the mores of his own tribe as though he were some visiting inspector. It was as if Margaret Mead had been a South Sea Islander. Yet, as E. M. Forster said, 'To talk about Crabbe is to talk about England. . . . He grew up among poor people, and he has been called their poet. But he did not like the poor. When he started writing, it was the fashion to pretend that they were happy shepherds and shepherdesses, who were always dancing, or anyhow had hearts of gold . . . but Crabbe's verdict on the working classes is unfavourable. And when he comes to the richer and more respectable . . . he remains sardonic, and sees them as poor people who haven't been found out. . . . To all of them, and to their weaknesses, he extends a little pity, a little contempt, a little cynicism, and a much larger portion of reproof. The bitternesses of his early experiences had eaten into his soul. . . .'

During the summer of 1787, soon after Crabbe had published *The Village*, another country poet, William Cowper, for whom this had been a miserable, worrying year and who, to keep the Black Dog at bay was reading anything and everybody, read at last the poems by Robert Burns which, for months, had been astonishing the literary world. Burns was twenty-eight and a ploughman, albeit on his brother's farm. Working a little Scottish farm was as penurious then as it was to be in the 1920s, when many a younger brother, tired of being the unpaid family hired-hand, emigrated to East Anglia, to fall upon those stagnant but promising acres and make his fortune. Robert Burns's object in publishing his poems was not to celebrate his oneness with the village of Mossgeil but to make enough money to get off the land altogether and to sail to Jamaica and work on

a plantation. Cowper read these now-famous poems with
bewilderment. In fact . . . 'I have read them *twice*; and though
they be written in a language that is new to me . . . I think
them, on the whole, a very extraordinary production. He is,
I believe, the only poet these kingdoms have produced in the
lower rank of life, since Shakespeare . . . who need not be
indebted for any part of his praise to a charitable consideration
of his origin, and the disadvantages under which he has
laboured. It will be a pity hereafter if he should not divest
himself of barbarism, and content himself with writing pure
English. . . . *He who can command admiration dishonours himself if
he aims no higher than to raise a laugh. . . .*'

William Cowper, that gentlest, kindest of men and one who
lived in the deep Buckinghamshire countryside with all the
charity, simplicity and good taste of a Mr. Knightley, and is
as far from being a Sweet Auburn tyrant as could be imagined,
remains none the less a devotee of the Augustan doctrine of rural
harmony and neo-classical order. Although he cannot avoid the
fact that Robert Burns is a genius, neither can he avoid the
implications of that wild free language. And so, with a terribly
similar reflex action to that of the Helpstone villagers when
confronted by John Clare, Cowper laughs.

Cowper's feeling for the countryside was the purest distillation
of the old conservative attitudes—those same attitudes which
still flow through so much of the vast literature we annually
produce to congratulate ourselves on our rural basis. A writer
can let himself go on the iniquities of the city but the village
remains critically sacrosanct.

Cowper's *Letters*, in which village joy and sorrow are so
perfectly conveyed, was John Constable's favourite book,
and he died with it in his hand. The greatest painter of the
English Romantic Movement was a revolutionary on canvas
only, and the superb series of Suffolk river-side paintings
which he created during the years immediately following
Waterloo, and which have since been called 'the landscape of
every English mind', were, in effect, a marvellous apologia for
Tory-Augustan 'order', as well as being 'true to Nature',
Looking at them now, it is impossible to believe that while they
were being produced, labourers rioted and were lighting
bonfires on the hills, that on one occasion at least things had
got so out of hand that both the squire and rector had fled,
and that Captain Swing was in the neighbourhood. Constable
himself travelled constantly from Soho to Dedham to refresh

himself at the 'fountain-head', as he called it, of all he worshipped and understood. To him, the pattern of life in the
Stour Valley, an eighteenth-century creation so far as he could
appreciate it, was a divine one.

Post-war famine, Enclosure, and the strange, unknown
pressures brought about by the Industrial Revolution were
behind the disorders of East Bergholt. The 1817 map of the
village on which its inhabitants stated their claims before
Enclosure, shows that all John Constable claimed was the
cottage he bought, while still a boy, to turn into a studio. But
many, as elsewhere, were unable to claim anything because
of illiteracy or ignorance, and were made paupers. When
Constable heard of the sufferings of these villagers, he sent
blankets from London, that basic charitable gesture. But when
he heard that the Suffolk and Essex labourers were forming
protective unions—those little men who carry on with their
quiet tasks in his great pictures—he was shocked and angry.
Archdeacon Fisher, his friend, had a more sympathetic attitude.
He and his family were virtually isolated by thousands of starving country people. While he saw their desperate attempts to
band themselves together as a natural reaction to the disaster
which was engulfing them, Constable, on the other hand, saw
them only as an evil menace to the God-ordained pattern
of rural life. His warnings to Archdeacon Fisher were harsh
and to the point. 'Remember that I know these people well.
There are no such corrupt hordes as any set of mechanics who
work in a shop together as a party. . . .' A century and a half
later the Agricultural Workers' Union is still looked at by some
as something which the beautiful British countryside could well
do without.

Meanwhile, as the 'union' workhouses went up, to the best
Benthamite designs, to shelter large numbers of displaced
peasants, the scenery Constable worshipped intensified its
spiritual hold over him. 'Nothing can exceed the beauty of the
country', he wrote. 'It makes pictures seem trumpery.'

When the long peace between the gentlemen and the
peasants was broken by the rationalization of what remained
of the manorial system, the contrast between the two rural
cultures was often so extreme that the baronet in his park could
feel that he was surrounded, not so much by his countrymen as
by savages. The work forces were moving towards the time when
they no longer possessed faces, only 'hands'. 'Osbert', remarked
Sir George Sitwell, staring across Sheffield, 'do you realize

that there is nobody between us and the Locker-Lampsons?'
Even good Archdeacon Fisher told Constable that it wasn't
because he and his wife had to run a private welfare state for
a great tract of Berkshire that he was so depressed, it was
because 'there is nobody we can meet'. Both he and Constable
continued to revel in the new concepts of Nature as described
by Wordsworth. 'Every step I take, and to whatever object
I turn my eye,' said the artist, 'that sublime expression in the
Scriptures, "I am the resurrection and the life", seems verified
about me,'—except, that is, when he caught sight of the
inhabitants of this beautiful country, when he was obliged
to add, 'The poor people are dirty and to approach one of the
cottages is almost insufferable.'

The threat to the idyll flutters nervously—though usually
so slightly that it escapes ordinary detection—in the novels
of Jane Austen. And, of course, being Jane Austen, she puts
it to good comic use, no more so than when, in *Emma*, she
allows that peerless girl to wed Mr. Knightley because his
presence in the house will be an added protection against
someone who is stealing hens from the hen-run. Why, it may be
asked, is Mr. Woodhouse so jumpy? Why did 'poor Miss
Taylor', by marrying Mr. Weston and going off to live in a
house only *half a mile* from Hartfield, create such difficulties?
Emma, who is only nineteen and in flourishing health, had once
walked to the Westons, 'but it was not pleasant'. *Why* wasn't it
pleasant? When Harriet Smith and her schoolfriend, two other
excessively healthy teenage ladies, had taken a walk and
encountered a gypsy family, they behaved as hysterically as
though they had run into cannibals. Why? When Jane Fairfax
is seen strolling by herself across the meadows to the post office,
the consequent consternation concerning her safety could not
have been greater had she been making off for 'Swisser-
land'. Critics have dwelt upon the hermetic quality of Jane
Austen's country society, 'Two or three families', etc., being
her ideal recipe for fiction, but what really lies behind all this
witty terror of the ordinary agriculture background? Jane
Austen's interpretation of Augustanism is to present the park as
Paradise. It is unnatural or unwise to wish to leave, or to leave,
Paradise. Although London is only sixteen miles away from
Hartfield, Emma has never been there. Nor has she ever seen
the sea, which is also near. ('The sea is rarely any use to anybody', says her father.) Mrs. Elton's real sin is not her vulgarity
as such but her blasphemy in taking a short cut to the park

(Paradise), for as Mr. Elton's bride she has to be received by its jealous denizens. She has bounced straight from the rooms above a Bristol warehouse to holy Hartfield without going through any of the purifying disciplines essential to such a great spiritual advance. Her 'I think I go first', when dinner is served; and her 'Knightley', when she addresses the individual about whom everybody else can say 'That you might not see one in a hundred, with *gentleman* so plainly written in', is not only cheek, it is hubris.

The novel's climaxes are created by the author's allowing this delicious county Paradise to make moral collisions with the sane heart of the English countryside as she recognized it. The scene in which a young working farmer is thought 'too low' for silly Harriet by proud Emma, and then turns out to be the *friend* of Mr. Knightley himself, is one of many which steady the comic impulse in this, the wittiest novel in the language. The laughter in Jane Austen's villages is always at the expense of dishonesty and affectation, the tears at the threat of destruction of any part of a unique rural civilization.

But if Harriet's young farmer is so low that Emma has to include him in the yeomanry, which is 'precisely the order of people with whom I feel I can have nothing to do', what hope of salvation is there for Hodge himself? None—in the literary sense—beyond those utilitarian appearances when either he or his wife clump by on the way to toil. No wonder that the poor creature bursts out laughing at the charades which are supposed to be going on above his head, so to speak. Now and then they go on a bit more than he can bear, and then he lets fly. William Hazlitt heard such an outburst with shock and disbelief at the extraordinary effect it had on him. He was used to mockery— Barry Cornwall said that 'Hazlitt was crowned with deformation' but he hardly expected it from this quarter.

His favourite hide-out was Winterslowe, the Wiltshire village introduced to him by Sarah Stoddart, his uncomfortable wife, and the proto-New Woman. There Hazlitt's own special concept of rural bliss—lying on his back on a sunny hillside, doing absolutely nothing—could be indulged while Sarah hiked. But one fatal day he read a book while drinking in the village pub and something was said, and then somebody laughed. For an ugly moment the lettered and the unlettered out-stared each other from their incommunicable solitudes. Then Hazlitt the radical, the eloquent defender of the village people of England against the horrible proposals of the

Reverend Mr. Malthus, unleashed such a tirade against country loutishness as no squarson could even have imagined:

'All country people hate each other!' he declared. 'They have so little comfort, that they envy their neighbours the small pleasures or advantage, and nearly grudge themselves the necessities of life. From not being accustomed to enjoyment, they become hardened and averse to it—stupid, for want of thought, selfish for want of society. There is nothing good to be had in the country, or if there is, they will not let you have it. They had rather injure themselves than oblige anyone else. Their common mode of life is a system of wretchedness and self-denial, like what we read of among barbarous tribes. You live out of the world. . . . You cannot do a single thing you like; you cannot walk out or sit at home, or write or read, or think or look as if you did, without being subject to impertinent curiosity. The apothecary annoys you with his complaisance, the parson with his superciliousness. If you are poor you are despised; if you are rich you are feared and hated. If you do anyone a favour, the whole neighbourhood is up in arms; the clamour is that of a rookery. . . . There is a perpetual round of mischiefmaking and backbiting for want of any better amusement. . . . There are no shops, no taverns, no theatres, no opera, no concerts, no pictures . . . no books or knowledge of books. Vanity and luxury are the civilisers of the world, and sweeteners of human life. Without objects either of pleasure or action, it grows harsh and crabbed. The mind becomes stagnant, the affections callous. . . . Man left to himself soon degenerates into a very disagreeable person. Ignorance is always bad enough, but *rustic* ignorance is intolerable. . . . The benefits of knowledge are never so well understood as from seeing the effects of ignorance, *in their naked, undisguised state*, upon the common country people. Their selfishness and insensibility are perhaps less owing to the hardships and privations, which make them, like people out at sea in a boat, ready to devour one another, than to their having no idea of anything beyond themselves and their immediate sphere of action. . . . Persons who are in the habit of reading novels . . . are compelled to take a deep interest in . . . the thoughts and feelings of people they never saw. . . . Books, in Lord Bacon's phrase, 'are a discipline of humanity'. Country people have none of these advantages . . . and so they amuse themselves by fancying the disasters and disgraces of their particular acquaintance. Having no humpbacked Richard to excite their wonder and abhorrence, they make themselves a bugbear . . . out of the first obnoxious person they can lay their hands on. . . . All their spare time is spent in manufacturing the lie for the day. . . . The common people in civilized countries are a kind of domesticated savage. They have not the wild imagination, the passions, the fierce energies, or dreadful vicissitudes of the savage tribes, nor have they the leisure, the indolent enjoyments and romantic superstitions which belong to the pastoral life in milder climates. *They are taken out of a state of nature, without being put in possession of the refinements of art.'*

Invective aside, there was plenty of truth in Hazlitt's rage. Lost, that was what the country people of England were in 1817, when this censure of them appeared. The condemnation was published just a few months after *Emma* and at the very moment when John Constable had begun the marvellous series of Stour Valley landscapes, each with its sprinkling of miniscule boatmen and field-workers, with which he hoped to establish himself in the eyes of the Royal Academy. And also during the period which saw the publication of Crabbe's last poems. Byron thought Crabbe's subject-matter 'coarse and impractical', and the majority of people found the workaday village life of Constable's paintings 'too low' to hang in their drawing-rooms. As for John Clare, those whose taste for rural life had been conditioned by schoolroom immersions in Virgil and Homer, and later lessons from *The Seasons*, or even by William Wordsworth, saw in this great poet little more than a clumsy kind of precocity.

In 1871—the beginning of the decade in which there was a disastrous combination of great rains and efficient grain-ships from the Canadian and American ports through which poured the harvests from fabulous prairie farms—rural England slipped once more into depression. Its agriculture was literally washed out and, except for brief Government protection during the First World War, was to remain so until the 1940s. Country people fled in their hundreds of thousands from the stagnant scene. They went into the railways, into service, into factories, to the colonies and into limbo. All this while the land itself began to receive a new veneration, this time from the tycoons of the Industrial Revolution who needed a great many acres of it in order to support the titles which began to come their way during the 1880s. Their efforts to assimilate the rural-based culture of the old landed families created much of the drama in late Victorian fiction.

It was in 1871 that Tinsley the publisher put out a mystifying novel called *Desperate Remedies*. The reviews were mixed, as they say. The story was anonymous but contained such expert descriptions of girls getting dressed that the general opinion was that the author was a woman. The novel was also found to be 'disagreeable' and 'full of crimes', although some critics were able to trace in it a new kind of 'awe' and noticed that the

'humble actors' exhibited powers which had 'previously been
ignored in peasant society'. Thomas Hardy, who was thirty-
one, read the worst of these reviews, that in the *Spectator*, while
perched on a Dorset stile, and the bitterness remained with him
until the end of his life. The decision to forsake architecture for
literature had been hard, and immediately after posting off
Desperate Remedies to the publisher he had gloomily underlined
in his copy of *Hamlet* the words: 'Thou woulds't not think how
ill all's here about my heart: but it is no matter!' It was certainly
a more tentative summing-up of his literary temerity than
Clare's, who at the end was able to say,

> A silent man in life's affairs
> A thinker from a boy,
> A peasant in his daily cares,
> A poet in his joy.

A few weeks later, this time while reading Smith and Son's
remainder list on Exeter station, Thomas Hardy found
Desperate Remedies offered at 2s. 6d. and was so upset that he
wrote to Macmillan's, to whom he had sent another novel,
Under the Greenwood Tree, demanding the return of his manuscript. He would, he told his sweetheart in Cornwall, 'banish
novel-writing for ever'.

Then, pragmatically for one who was to be such a key figure
in the unification of the lettered and the unlettered cultures of
England, Hardy set about earning his living designing buildings
for London School Board. All the same, *Under the Greenwood
Tree*, with its hero based upon the man who brought the
author's father his building materials, was published a year later;
and now both critics and readers began what was to be the
slow, touchy, self-examining process of allowing ordinary village
people access to the passion, imagination, feeling and eloquence
previously reserved for the parks and rectories. For a short
period these disconcerting country forces revealed by Hardy
managed to entertain the public with their quaint customs and
displays of rustic love; but soon, as with George Crabbe, less
bearable sights began to intrude. Extraordinary crimes, sex,
fatal pressures, pagan strengths which showed no sign of ever
having been conquered by Christian ethics. The style, too, was
upsetting—'Like sand in honey', Richard le Gallienne called it.
And reviewer after reviewer began to echo Cowper's stricture on
Burns—'It will be a pity hereafter if he should not divest himself
of barbarism and content himself with writing pure English.'

Many years later, when Hardy had become accepted, Havelock-Ellis made an interesting comment on his success. He said that 'the real and permanent interest in Hardy's books is not his claim to be an exponent of Wessex—i.e. the rural workers—but his intense preoccupation with the mysteries of women's hearts'. And Havelock-Ellis goes on to say that what Hardy was finally engaged in, most completely and impermissibly in *Jude the Obscure*, was bringing the instinctive, spontaneous and unregarded aspects of Nature even closer to the rigid routines of human life, making it *more* human (or inhuman); *more* moral (or immoral). Hardy was also emphasizing the unconciousness in Nature of everything except her essential law, and he was not in sympathy with a society which believed that it could live according to rules which did not take this law into account. It was the clash between Nature and 'society' which made the necessary conflict in Hardy the writer.

'This conflict', continues Havelock-Ellis, 'reaches its highest point around women. Truly or falsely, for good or for evil, woman has always been for man the supreme priestess, or the supreme devil, of Nature. "A woman," says Proudhon—himself the incarnation of the revolt of Nature in the heart of man—'even the most charming and virtuous woman, always contains an element of cunning, the wild beast element. She is a tamed animal that sometimes returns to her natural instinct. This cannot be said in the same degree of man." The loving student of the elemental in Nature so becomes the loving student of women, the sensitive historian of her conflicts with "sin" and with "repentance"—the creations of man. Not, indeed, that any woman who has "sinned", if her sin was love, ever really "repents". It is probable that a true experience of the one emotional state as of the other remains a little foreign to her, "*Sin* having probably been the invention of men who never really knew what love is".'

You will see that we have come a long way from *The Seasons*. You will also see that John Clare and Angel Clare have shares in the same profound rural consciousness.

In 1883 Richard Jefferies published that strange essay *The Story of My Heart* which Elizabeth Jennings rightly sees as a non-Christian equivalent of the mystic abstractions of Traherne. As with Hardy, Jefferies repudiates that a countryside shares the opinions of the human beings who happen to be living in it. By one of those strange coincidences, *The Story of*

My Heart appeared at the very same time as John Constable's paintings, which might sound odd. But Constable had died in 1837 leaving some eight hundred unsold, unwanted pictures; and these had remained, hidden and more or less ignored, until half a century later the best of them were given to the nation by his daughter. Thus Constable's superb apology for Augustan harmony, whose claims he had so brilliantly strengthened by his scientific approach to Nature and his revolutionary impressionistic brushwork, burst its way into the country-worshipping hearts of the British at the same moment as the villages had found their native voice. For John Constable, the trees, fields, flowers, rivers and, most of all, the skies, lived and moved in concord with the noblest human motives. For Jefferies and Hardy, such things were 'a force without a mind'.

'There is nothing human in Nature', said Jefferies. 'The earth would let me perish on the ground. . . . Burning in the sky the great sun, of whose company I have been so fond, would merely burn on and make no motion to assist me. The trees care nothing for us: the hill I visited so often in days gone by has not missed me. This very thyme which scents my fingers did not grow for that purpose, but its own. . . . By night it is the same as day: the stars care not, and we are nothing to them. . . . *If the entire human race perished at this hour, what difference would it make to the earth?'*

Such statements wrung much of the contentment out of the simple life and helped to suggest a threatening amoral landscape which Edwardian Hellenists—including E. M. Forster, Saki, and Forrest Reid—peopled with forsaken Pans and other brooding and resentful stream and woodland deities.

Thomas Hardy himself became angry when his anti-euphoric view of country life was constantly put down to his pessimism. 'All this talk about my pessimism! What does it matter what an author's view of life is? If he finally succeeds in conveying a completely satisfying artistic expression, that is what counts.'

All the same, it *was* the cosmic brutality in his work which, among other things, caused the twentieth-century 'country writer' to try and avoid the excesses of both too much moral illumination and too much pounding darkness. Such avoidances have, of course, led to a stream of innocuous rural *belle-lettrism* unequalled throughout the world and to new versions of the idyll. But they have also led to many of the most serious statements of modern literature. When I think of village literature I think of *Four Quartets* as well as *Lark Rise to Candleford*.

All post-Hardy writing needs to be assessed against a remarkable work published in 1902, *Rural England*, by Sir Henry Rider Haggard, a Norfolk farmer who usually wrote novels. This is a brilliant, factual, statistical, and apolitical account of the social effects of the last great agricultural depression at, more or less, its midway mark. The author chose a text from the *Book of Judges* with which to introduce his county-by-county analysis: 'The highways were unoccupied . . . the inhabitants of the villages ceased.' Reading *Rural England* now it seems scarcely sane that Britain, then able to command an almost inexhaustible wealth, could have permitted such a disaster to have run its course, blighting both the land and those who lived on it. The indifference and callousness shown towards the agricultural workers in particular, many of whom were starving, was appalling. The legacy of this neglect haunts the shires to this day.

Curiously, it was from this wretched scene that the conservationists feverishly began to retrieve a culture which was no longer regarded as belonging to boors but to the essential heart of Britain itself. The Folk-Lore and Folk-Song and Folk-Dance societies copied tirelessly. Dialect experts listened with respect to accents which they knew to be those of Beowulf, Caedman, Langland, Chaucer, Shakespeare, Johnson and Tennyson. Now conservation of rural culture has grown until it includes conservation of the entire country scene itself. The cottage which Constable found too disgusting to enter in 1820, and which Rider Haggard found deserted and in ruins in 1902, is now 'desirable'. The poor crooked spade hangs safely in the Rural Industries Museum. Everything belonging to the village now belongs to our higher nature. Those who threaten thatch, hedge or peace are now the barbarians. And it is John Clare's village, not Thomson's, which provides the standards for this idyll. The village of the villagers. It is often said that the conservationists of this village are the middle-classes but they are, in most instances, the grandchildren.

TREDEGAR MEMORIAL LECTURE

This lecture perpetuates the memory of the first Viscount Tredegar, of the Second Creation. It was founded by his son, a Fellow of the Society from 1928 until 1949.

WILLIAM BECKFORD, PRINCE OF AMATEURS

By BRIAN FOTHERGILL, F.S.A., F.R.S.L.

(Read 22 March 1973)

John Guest, M.A., F.R.S.L., in the Chair

I SUPPOSE that William Beckford is chiefly remembered as being the author of an oriental fantasy, as the builder of a gothic folly with a tower that certainly fell down twice and possibly three times during his life-time, and as a man of vast, almost legendary inheritance; 'England's wealthiest son' as Byron called him. His was the sort of life around which legends tend to gather, even without the encouragement that Beckford himself sometimes gave to the stories that circulated about him. His habit of seclusion created an atmosphere of mystery, and it was easy to imagine that Fonthill Abbey was the scene of vague orgies rather than the sanctuary of quiet and secluded study that was in fact, for most of the time, very much nearer the truth.

Beckford had been ostracized as the result of a scandal, or rather on the mere suspicion of scandalous behaviour, when he was only in his mid-twenties. Society continued to shun him for the rest of his life but at the same time retained an eager curiosity about all that he did; and when he retired to his abbey and surrounded his estate with a twelve-foot high wall with seven gates always kept locked and guarded to keep out unwelcome intruders, it was only natural that people should draw the worst possible conclusions as to what went on on the other side of the wall.

Had they known that behind it there lived a man who always rose early, took vigorous exercise on horseback, passed his time in scholarly pursuits and was usually in bed by ten o'clock at night, no doubt they would have been bitterly disappointed. It is true that he did have some peculiarities; he hated the hunting of wild animals and had always wanted to be a writer, two predilections highly suspect in an English gentleman in the eighteenth century.

For the public at large he held a sort of fascination, a glamour that sprang from his curious circumstances, his wealth, his unusual talents, and the taint of scandal that he never entirely succeeded in eradicating. His abbey was known to be the very opposite of austere. It contained a renowned collection of pictures and works of art as well as manuscripts and books. He had purchased Edward Gibbon's library and had a discerning eye for old masters. Out of his collection, in spite of Hazlitt's sneer that he had neither feeling nor imagination in his choice of pictures, nine how hang in the National Gallery in London, two in the Metropolitan Museum in New York, and one in the National Gallery in Berlin. Everyone who knew of Fonthill Abbey was eager to examine its interior and inspect the collections it contained, but no one wished to meet its owner; such a confrontation might be altogether too compromising.

To understand this curious position in which Beckford stood it is necessary to look at his life as well as his writings, for each reflected the other to an extraordinary degree.

Beckford was born on 29 September 1760, and was thus forty-three years younger than Horace Walpole and twenty-eight years older than Byron, to name two men to whom he is sometimes compared. He was to survive Byron by twenty years. He was born (to paraphrase Oscar Wilde) in the purple of commerce on his father's side and sprang from the ranks of the aristocracy on his mother's.

His father was Alderman Beckford, a Wilkesian Whig who is famous for the rebuke he administered to George III, an act of *lèse-majesté* that he survived by only three weeks. The origins of the family are obscure but can be traced to a tailor who plied his trade in Maidenhead towards the middle of the seventeenth century, an ancestor to whom William did not care to draw much attention. The tailor's descendants moved to Jamaica where they amassed a great fortune out of sugar and slavery. Beckford's great-grandfather is supposed to have left a strong-box which when opened after his death was discovered to contain the larger part of a million pounds in cash. I say 'supposed' because the story is probably not true, but that such stories could be told and believed gives an indication of the sort

of sums associated with the name of Beckford. Certainly when
the Alderman was Lord Mayor of London he was said to have
entertained on a more lavish scale than any predecessor in
office since the reign of Henry VIII.

The elder Beckford did not marry until he was in his fifties.
Before that he had consoled himself in other ways and was the
father of seven or eight illegitimate children. His wife was
Maria Hamilton, granddaughter of an Earl of Abercorn and
descended in three lines from Edward III. Her son William, who
like his mother was a snob, found this much more interesting
than his descent from the tailor of Maidenhead. All his life
Beckford was fascinated by genealogy, and much of his time
was spent in drawing up family trees and laying claim to
escutcheons with which to emblazon the painted windows of
Fonthill Abbey. In this way he made the gratifying discovery
that he was descended, not from one, but from all the barons
who had signed Magna Carta. For him genealogy was an art
rather than a science.

The wealth of Beckford's father and the aristocratic con-
nections on his mother's side marked him out for a political
career. His godfather was the great Earl of Chatham and the
family owned two parliamentary boroughs, while the Alderman
himself had sat as M.P. for the City of London. But because of
his delicate health the boy was not given the conventional
education of a budding politician.

Instead of going to a public school he was educated at home
by tutors. Even so, the very best were provided for him. He was
taught the principles of architecture by Sir William Chambers
and drawing by the water-colour painter Alexander Cozens.
It was always Beckford's boast that he had been taught music
by Mozart, and this was true; but it should be pointed out that
he was only five years old at the time and the Master no more
than nine.

It is interesting to note in relation to the future author of
Vathek that both Chambers and Cozens had experience of the
east. Chambers had actually been to China; and Cozens, who
had been born in Russia and was said to be a natural son of
Peter the Great, had travelled extensively and come in contact
with Persians and other orientals. Beckford was fascinated to
hear tales of distant eastern lands and quickly fell under
Cozen's rather sinister spell, for it has been suggested that the
painter was responsible for interesting his pupil in magic as well
as oriental history.

Alderman Beckford died when his son and heir was only ten years old. This was undoubtedly a misfortune for the boy who was deprived of the down-to-earth influence of a strong-willed father and thrown more completely into the protective care of an anxious and over-possessive mother. By his father's death he became a millionaire; one of the richest subjects in Europe.

He was thus very much surrounded by feminine influences in his childhood. His mother's friends tended to have strongly evangelical views and were referred to by her son as 'methodistical dowagers'. Their influence, severe and Calvinistic, was at variance with the world of imagination inspired by Cozen's tales and such reading as the *Arabian Nights* in which, we are told, Beckford indulged at a time of life 'when other children are seldom of an age to do more than comprehend their letters'. In this atmosphere he grew up to be precocious, introspective, solitary, and subject to fits of violent temper when unable to get his own way.

Beckford was considered too exotic and delicate a flower for the harsh atmosphere of an English university. Instead, like Gibbon, though for different reasons, he was sent to Geneva when he was seventeen and remained there for a year. He had already made a first attempt at writing in his skit *Biographical Memoirs of Extraordinary Painters* and had started on a story, never finished, which was later published as *The Vision*. The painters in the first book are imaginary, and it was said to have been inspired by listening to the malapropisms of the housekeeper at Fonthill as she showed visitors round the picture gallery. It shows Beckford's sense of humour which was always one of his saving graces. *The Vision*, not published until 1930, gives the first indication of the imaginative powers that were later to flourish in *The History of the Caliph Vathek*.

It was at this period that Beckford wrote a sort of manifesto which he sent to Cozens from Geneva. It shows his attitude of revolt against the conventional standards of his class and explains, perhaps, why his mother had decided to send him to Geneva and not to Cambridge or Oxford. 'To receive visits and to return them,' he wrote, 'to be mighty civil, well-bred, quiet, prettily dressed and smart is to be what your old ladies call in England a charming Gentleman and what those of the same stamp abroad know by the appellation of *un homme comme il faut*. Such an animal how often am I doomed to be. . . . To despise poetry and venerable Antiquity, murder Taste, abhor imagination, detest all the charms of Eloquence unless capable of mathematical Demonstration, and more than all to be vigorously incredulous, is to gain the reputation of good sound Sense. Such an animal I am sometimes doomed to be! To glory in Horses, to know how to knock up and how to cure them, to smell of the stable, swear, talk bawdy, eat roast beef, drink, speak bad French, go to Lyons and come back again with manly disorders, are qualifications not despicable in the Eyes of the English here. Such an animal I am determined not to be! Were I not to hear from you sometimes, see a Genius or two sometimes, to go to Voltaire's sometimes, and to the Mountains very often, I should die.' Beckford, we can see, was already at seventeen or eighteen a Romantic, and was to remain one for the rest of his long life.

He returned to England in 1778, his character firmly set in the romantic mould and his pen in full command of its idiom. Back at Fonthill he recorded in his diary: 'The Dusk approaches. I am musing on the Plain before the House which my Father reared. No cheerful illuminations appear in the Windows, no sounds of Musick issue from the Porticos, no gay Revellers rove carelessly along the Colonnades, but all is dark, silent and abandoned. Such Circumstances suit the present tone of my mind. . . .'

It was in this mood of self-concious melancholy that the young man was sent on a round of country-house visits. The idea was to divert him from his morbid state of mind. Instead, however, of coming back more like the beef-eating young men whom he so much despised, the tour was to result in an encounter which was later to be responsible for his social downfall.

At Powderham Castle in Devonshire he met the eleven-year-old William Courtenay and immediately formed a strong emotional attachment to him. The boy, who later became the 19th Earl of Devon, was a pampered child, the only son in a family of thirteen girls, and had earned for himself the nickname of 'Kitty' Courtenay. Beckford's attachment, though morbidly romantic, was certainly otherwise quite innocent at this time and possibly always remained so, but he took no precautions to conceal the strength of his feelings for Courtenay and made every effort to keep in touch with his young friend when the visit to Powderham came to an end.

His attachment to Courtenay, though strongly romantic, was not exclusive of other emotions, and at this period of his life he was certainly attracted to the opposite sex, though he seems to have had a predilection for women older than himself. One such was Louise, wife of his cousin Peter Beckford, with whom he was to have an amorous friendship for some years. She very much encouraged the more exotic side of his personality, even to the extent of aiding and sympathizing with him in his infatuation for Courtenay.

In 1780, probably in the hope of extricating him from both of these entanglements, Beckford was sent on the Grand Tour, and made his first acquaintance with Italy. In Naples he stayed with Sir William Hamilton, who was his mother's first cousin, and in Lady Hamilton found one of the few people who were to give him understanding and sympathetic advice. This was of course Sir William's first wife, not the boisterous Emma whom Beckford secretly detested and later described as 'the Cleopatra who proved the bane of our most triumphal admiral and fixed a foul and sanguine spot upon his glorious memory'. The first Lady Hamilton brought a calm influence to bear on his spirit, genuinely entered into his problems, offering him sound and acceptable guidance. Unfortunately, her early death shortly after Beckford's return home removed this one steadying influence from his life.

While he was on his travels Beckford kept a diary which, when he returned, he worked up into a book. It was a subjective, impressionistic record of his travels, moods, thoughts and reflections, and was published under the title of *Dreams, Waking Thoughts, and Incidents.* Its appearance caused his family the greatest alarm. How, they asked themselves, could he be launched on a political career as the author of a book which began: 'Shall I tell you my dreams? To give an account of my time is doing, I assure you, but little else. . . .' The young author was prevailed upon to suppress the edition and most of the copies were burnt. His mother and her advisers could only see a political future placed in jeopardy. It never occurred to them that they were smothering a creative talent. Fortunately the book was not completely lost, and it formed the basis of his later travel book *Italy, with Sketches of Spain and Portugal,* which was not published until 1834.

In spite of his family's encouragement Beckford faced the prospect of a political career with a total lack of enthusiasm, while his artistic temperament felt stifled for want of expression. 'Which way can I turn?' he asked Lady Hamilton in a letter of 1781. 'Public affairs I dare not plunge into. My health is far too wavering. Whilst I write, my hand trembles like that of a paralytic Chinese. Strange colours swim before my eyes and sounds

keep ringing in my ears for which I can hardly account. . . .
For ambitious spirits this is not the time to shrink out of the
way. Dangers and difficulties are their pavements. But I no
longer feel myself bold enough to tread such monsters under
foot. Once upon a time I fancied myself filled with ambitions.
I looked this morning and could find not a grain.'

Beckford sought relief in his dilemma by plunging into the
celebrations for his coming-of-age, which were carried out with
an opulence that befitted the richest commoner in England.
But these public rejoicings only held half of his interest; now that
he was his own master he meant to celebrate the occasion in his
own peculiar way with a party for his particular circle of friends.

This took place at Christmas time, 1781, three months after
his twenty-first birthday. The setting was the great house
nicknamed 'Fonthill Splendens' which the Alderman had built
after a previous house had been destroyed by fire in 1754.
Chief among the guests were Louisa Beckford and her cousin
Sophia (described by Beckford himself as 'perhaps the most
beautiful woman in England'), the sinister Cozens, and 'Kitty'
Courtenay, then about thirteen or fourteen years old. 'Careworn
visages were ordered to keep aloof,' Beckford later wrote,
'no sunk-in mouths or furroughed foreheads were permitted to
meet our eyes. Our society was extremely youthful and lovely
to look upon.'

The whole great mansion was sealed off from the outside
world, all doors and windows screened to exclude the light of
common day. The interior of the house had been decorated
especially for the party by Philip de Loutherbourg, the artist
and scene painter, who produced magic effects by the mani-
pulation of coloured glass and gauze in front of lamps, creating
what Beckford approvingly described as 'necromantic light'.
The effect he declared was that of 'a Demon Temple deep
beneath the earth, set apart for tremendous mysteries'. In
this curiously artificial world he and his guests remained for
three days.

In another passage of his account of this party Beckford
wrote: 'The solid Egyptian Hall looked as if hewn out of living
rock—the line of apartments and apparently endless passages
extending from it on either side were all vaulted—an intermin-
able staircase, which when you looked down it, appeared as
deep as the well in the pyramid, and when you looked up, was
lost in vapour, led to suits of stately apartments gleaming with
marble pavements, as polished as glass.'

This secret gathering behind locked doors, which was soon to give rise to lurid rumours, was the work of a young man who had protested to a friend upon becoming twenty-one: 'I'm still in my cradle! Spare the delicacy of my infantile ears. Leave me to scamper on verdant banks—all too ready, alas, to crumble, but rainbow-tinted and flower-strewn.' His character showed a strange conjunction of sophistication with a reluctance to grow up and face the responsibilities of his position; a puzzling mixture of immaturity and precocity. This was to remain the same all his life, and he never fully out-grew his longing for the symbolical innocence of those flower-strewn banks.

Beckford's account of the effects produced at Fonthill Splendens on this occasion prefigure the later description of the halls of Eblis in *The History of the Caliph Vathek*; the same subterranean cavern, the same 'stairway of polished marble', the same conception of 'rows of columns and arcades running off in diminishing perspective' that we discover in his Arabian tale. Work on the book, to which I will refer in a moment, in fact began in the following month, but it would seem that the ideas out of which it grew were already forming in his mind, and the party in December 1781 was an attempt to create for a brief moment in actual life what *Vathek* itself was to achieve in words.

This party of young people in the house from which all 'methodistical dowagers' and chaperons had been banished became the centre of a ripple of scandal that gradually spread through society. The rumour was that magical rites had been performed, a rumour (and it was no more) which sprang partly from garbled reports of de Loutherbourg's mysterious light effects and partly from the extravagant language used by Beckford and his friends which was full of references to magic, spells, and enchantments. The knowledge that Cozens had been present, so much older than the others and with his slightly baleful reputation, did little to set anxieties at rest.

It was the type of minor scandal that Beckford could easily have survived but to which people's minds returned when he was involved in a worse one. Certainly he did little to endear himself to people he met in society whom he thought to be dull or uninteresting, and he cultivated a gift for mimicry which he could use with deadly effect. In appearance he was small, with handsome features and striking eyes described as steel-grey. His voice was very high-pitched, like that of a eunuch, and he had a slightly feminine manner, especially when singing.

Indeed, one of his parlour tricks was to imitate the famous female opera singers of his day. In appearance, habit of mind, behaviour and opinions, this rich, arrogant, but fundamentally insecure young man struck people as being very decidedly exotic and un-English.

To his mother and family there seemed only one answer to this; he must be found a wife and a seat in parliament at the earliest possible moment. Beckford submitted quite calmly to both proposals. In May 1783 he rather unromantically married Lady Margaret Gordon, daughter of the 4th Earl of Aboyne. The marriage was to prove tragically brief but surprisingly happy. In 1784, having placed his own parliamentary boroughs at the disposal of the ministry, he took his seat as M.P. for Wells in Somerset. He had no interest whatsoever in House of Commons work and began negotiations almost at once to have himself raised to the peerage. During all this time he was constantly in communication with young William Courtenay, who was by now a boy at Westminster School.

The first hint of work on *Vathek* comes in a letter dated 21 January 1782, sent to the Revd. Samuel Henley, a master at Harrow and a student of Persian and Arabian literature, who was later to translate the book and publish it without the author's permission. 'The spirit has moved me this eve', Beckford wrote, 'and, shut up in my apartment as you advised, I have given way to fancies and inspirations, What will be the consequence of this mood I am not bold enough to determine.'

The result, as we know, was *The History of the Caliph Vathek* and the *Episodes* that form a sequel to it. Beckford later claimed that he wrote the main story in a single feverish effort of three days and two nights, and indeed he may well have prepared the first draft in that brief space of time; but altogether he spent a year working on the text until, on 13 January 1783, he was able to write to Henley: 'I go on bravely with the episodes of Vathek, and hope in a few days to wind up his adventures.'

One would like to say that *Vathek* occupies a unique place in the English language, but of course we are unable to do so because Beckford chose to write it in French. One reason why he did this was because it was consciously modelled in style, and to some extent in subject-matter, on Voltaire's *Zadig* and other oriental tales. While oriental themes were comparatively rare in English literature, they had had a certain vogue on the Continent for some time. Apart from Voltaire's work dating from the late 1740s, Carlo Gozzi's *Turandot* had been written

D

in 1762; and while Beckford was musing on his own oriental fantasy, his former master Mozart was recasting Bretzner's play *Belmont und Constanze* into his 'Turkish' opera *Die Entführung aus dem Serail*.

We must, however, look for another reason for Beckford's choice of language, and this we can discover not in his reading of continental authors or oriental originals, but in his innate snobbery. On 25 April 1782 he wrote to Henley: 'My Arabian tales go on prodigiously, and I think Count Hamilton will smile upon me when we are introduced to each other in Paradise.' Count Hamilton was, of course, Count Anthony Hamilton, a maternal ancestor of Beckford's, who not only wrote the memoirs of the Count de Grammont and other pieces, but wrote them all in French.

Finally there was a personal and more psychological reason for which Beckford himself was probably hardly aware. *Vathek* is a profoundly autobiographical and revealing document in which the temptations and conflicts that assailed the twenty-one-year-old author are reproduced and magnified on a tremendous scale. A note of adolescent despair runs though the whole story as we see the Caliph, whose character contains elements derived from both Beckford and his father, being led on inexorably to his terrible and inescapable doom, a fate which was (if I may remind you) the loss of 'the most precious gift of Heaven—*hope*'. It was a fate which the author saw in store for himself as well as his hero, with whom he identified completely, and he wrote in a foreign language, I believe, from an unconscious instinct of self-protection, even though he knew well enough that the French language was as familiar to most members of his social class as it was to himself.

The story of *Vathek* is the tale of a man caught in the prison of his own temperament and rushed headlong to destruction. There are moments of grace when the hero is offered the chance of redemption, but these are brushed aside and he is sped onwards to his doom. Finally, having reached the domain of Eblis, the Prince of Hell, and seen the treasures of the pre-adamite sultans, Vathek is condemned to wander for ever in the subterranean kingdom, his hand pressed to his side where beneath it his heart is consumed for ever by undying flames. He joins the multitude of lost souls who wander in complete silence through the halls. 'They were all as pale as corpses,' Beckford wrote, 'and their sunken eyes were like the phosphorescent lights which may be seen at nights in graveyards.

Some were plunged in profound meditation; while others, fuming with rage, ran hither and thither like tigers wounded by poisoned darts. Each avoided his fellows; and each, though he moved in the midst of a great concourse, wandered aimlessly as though he were alone.'

A feature employed by Beckford in this story is the tower which the Caliph builds 'through an insolent desire to penetrate the secrets of heaven'. It is not only the symbol of knowledge and power (both gained through disobedience to conventional wisdom), but it is a place of escape from the responsibilities of the world. It is also the centre from which emanate the wicked spells of the Caliph's mother, who is the evil genius of the book. This is Beckford's description of the Caliph's first ascent of his tower: 'His pride reached its height when he climbed for the first time the fifteen hundred steps of his tower, and looked down on the world below. Men seemed like ants, mountains like mole-hills, and [the city] itself like a beehive. The idea of his own greatness which this height gave him quite turned his head, and he was just about to begin worshipping himself when, raising his eyes, he saw that the stars seemed just as far away as they had been when he was on the ground. However, he consoled himself for the involuntary feeling of insignificance by thinking how great he would appear in the eyes of others; and besides, he flattered himself that the light of his understanding would travel far beyond the utmost limit of his vision, and would wrest from the stars the secrets of his fate.'

This is one of the clues to the self-identification of Beckford with his hero. Two years before starting work on his Arabian tale, he made the following note: 'My apartment shall be in the highest story of the tower . . . from whence I may observe the course of the planets and indulge my astrological fancies. Here I shall esteem myself under the peculiar influence of the stars.' Nearly ten years later, still obsessed by the same image, he wrote: 'I am growing rich and mean to build Towers, and sing hymns to the powers of Heaven on their summits, accompanied by almost as many sacbuts and psalteries as twanged round Nebuchadnezzar's image.' The result, as we know, was to be the great but unstable tower of Fonthill Abbey. It was for Beckford a symbol both of his revolt against society and his escape from its responsibilities; a refuge above the world from where he could contemplate the heavens and look down on the earth with a mixture of detachment and contempt.

Another interesting aspect of *Vathek* is the role of Carathis, the Caliph's mother. At the beginning of the story we learn that Vathek 'loved and respected her not only as a mother, but also as a woman endowed with very great talents'. But as the story unfolds she is revealed as being the very personification of evil. It is she who urges him on his fatal course, propitiates evil spirits on his behalf, and strengthens his resolve when his spirit of ill-doing flags.

Is this how Beckford now saw his mother, or is it merely a general revenge on the 'methodistical dowagers' and the restrictions they stood for in his life? Certainly his mother was busily engaged in preparing a course in life for him which he had no desire to follow, and was doing all in her power to discourage his artistic and literary hopes. It was she who had arranged his marriage as a counter-balance to the unwholesome attractions of 'Kitty' Courtenay and his like. But she hardly seemed to deserve the fate meted out to Vathek's evil mother at the end of the story. 'It is not thou who has led me into this hateful place,' the Caliph says to his companion in misfortune, 'it is the impious principles by which Carathis perverted my youth that have caused both my downfall and thine: oh that at least she might suffer with us.' His mother is then summoned before them and her heart consumed by fire with the other lost souls.

The story of *Vathek* was followed by the three *Episodes* which he wrote between 1783 and 1786. They were never published in his lifetime and indeed for a period were thought to be lost until they were rediscovered in the Charter Room of Hamilton Palace sixty-five years after Beckford's death. Each story tells how the narrator has found his way to the halls of Eblis and the subsequent loss of his soul, and in them Beckford explores the various less orthodox aspects of human relationships, including his own unfortunate affair with Courtenay. In this story on a pederastic theme propriety is saved in the nick of time when it is discovered that the boy prince Firouz has been a girl all the time, though after the discovery she loses no time in getting back into male dress again. In spite of this device it is in fact a story of homosexual love in which the young boy, or boy-girl, is represented as the corrupting influence who leads the elder man astray.

It would be interesting to know at exactly what time he wrote this particular tale, for it was during the period of the composition of the *Episodes* that the blow fell on Beckford himself and society turned its back on him for ever.

In the September and early October of 1784 he and his wife were staying again at Powderham Castle. Courtenay himself, now 17, was there with a party that included Lord Loughborough, who was Courtenay's uncle by marriage. What precisely happened is not known but Beckford and Courtenay were somehow discovered in a compromising situation and the story was allowed to find its way into the press. No authentic account of the episode has come down to us. What must be remembered is that no formal charge of any sort was ever brought against Beckford, and that the press attack on him, which was vicious in the extreme, was almost certainly inspired by Lord Loughborough whose wife had known Beckford before her marriage and had possibly been in love with him, and whose chief political rival was Beckford's own political patron Lord Chancellor Thurlow.

In spite of the lack of any formal charges the campaign that was worked up against Beckford meant his complete ruin as far as his place in society was concerned. His political career was finished. No more was heard of his peerage though his nomination to the House of Lords had been announced in the press and the letters patent for a barony were prepared. The whole of society buzzed with the scandal, sometimes with unconscious humour. To one of the clan of 'methodistical dowagers' his shocking fall from grace was attributed to what she called his ridiculous addiction to music, as a result of which, alas, 'all prospect of his becoming great or respectable was over'.

Beckford's wife stood nobly by him throughout the crisis though her brother did his best to persuade her to leave her husband. For a time the couple tried to brazen things out in England but after some months decided to go abroad. Here fate struck at him again, for in May 1786 Lady Margaret died after giving birth to their second daughter. Calumny, having found its tongue, could no longer remain silent where Beckford was concerned, and when the news of his wife's death reached England the newspapers put it about that she had died as a result of his brutal treatment of her. In fact his devotion to her was such that thirty years later, when he spoke of her to Samuel Rogers, the poet noticed that his eyes filled with tears.

This final attack was the last straw for him and filled him with a bitterness from which he never completely recovered. A few years later, the wound still unhealed, he wrote: 'Allowances were to be made for former attacks, but none for this, and I will own to you that the recollection of this black stroke fills me with

such horror and indignation that I sigh for the pestilential
breath of an African serpent to destroy every Englishman who
comes in my way.'

For the next few years Beckford spent most of his time abroad,
living rather like a prince in exile. According to the Irish peer
Lord Cloncurry he travelled with a cavalcade of 'about 30
horses with four carriages and a corresponding number of
servants'. On one occasion when the Emperor of Austria was
travelling incognito in the same area Beckford's entourage was
everywhere mistaken for that of the imperial party. But even
abroad the campaign against him was kept up. Cloncurry
reports that after Beckford's arrival in Switzerland 'letters
came from England . . . as a result of which our visits to
Beckford ceased', and in Lisbon the British minister refused to
present him at Court for the same reason.

To his second visit to Portugal in 1794 belongs his most
delightful book, the *Recollections of an Excursion to the Monasteries
of Alcobaça and Batalha*. It is not only one of the most entertaining short travel-books ever written, but in the opinion of
Mr. Boyd Alexander, our foremost Beckford authority, 'ever
since [its publication] he has been regarded as one of the best
describers of the Portuguese scene in any language'. It was based
on notes made at the time of his visit but not written until 1834,
when Beckford was seventy-four years old.

Some of the scenes portrayed in this book are well known,
like his account of the great monastic kitchen at Alcobaça, loaded
with game, venison and every sort of river fish as well as
vegetables and fruit of every variety. Beckford sums up the
reaction of the monks to this example of good living by quoting
the remark of the abbot: '"There," said my Lord Abbot, "we
shall not starve: God's bounties are great, it is fit we should
enjoy them."' These are the monks he later describes as 'no
wretched cadets of the mortification family, but true elder sons
of fat mother church'.

One passage, written by the elderly Beckford in recollection
of his earlier self, shows that his view of human nature had not
changed much since the days when he wrote *Vathek*: 'The
Prior ordered a fishing-party for our amusement; no great
amusement, however, for one who detests the sight of wretched
animals, inveigled from their cool aquatic homes, and cast on a
dry bank, gasping for life and distending their jaws in torment.
Full often have I fancied what woeful grimaces we children of
Adam would be compelled to make, should ever the colossal

inhabitants of a superior planet be permitted on some dread day of retribution to drop down on earth on an angling tour, and fish us out of our element for their dinner or recreation. No want of sport need be apprehended in this case—plenty would bite. Men have in general such wide-open appetites for the objects of their individual pursuits, that, only render the bait sufficiently tempting, and I promise they swallow it, hook and all. So few set any boundary to their voraciousness, that a shark might be chosen President of a Temperance Society with equal justice.'

After Beckford returned from his self-imposed exile he turned from writing to building. 'Some people drink to forget their unhappiness,' he wrote, 'I do not drink, I build.' From 1793 onwards his artistic energy became more and more absorbed in the building of Fonthill Abbey and later on of the Lansdowne Tower at Bath.

In the setting of these houses, in the seclusion forced on him by his social isolation and the peculiarities of his temperament, his life was devoted in its serious moments to study, collecting pictures, and the assembling of a large and important library. He was surrounded by servants, by his faithful Portuguese secretary and companion, by his dwarf, and by an army of workmen who toiled night and day for many years on the building of his tower and cloisters. The rest of the world left him very much alone; it was a splendid but sad existence. He died in May 1844 at the age of eighty-four, 'unrepentant, unreformed and immature', as Mr. Boyd Alexander has described him.

His literary output was small but of a unique character, and as far as *Vathek* and his travel-books are concerned, is still eminently readable. But he retained the attitude of a princely amateur and all too rarely rushed into print. One cannot help thinking that if Beckford had been a little bit poorer English literature might have been a good deal richer.

DON CARLOS COLOMA MEMORIAL LECTURE

This lecture perpetuates the memory of Don Carlos Coloma. It was founded by Dr. Olga Turner, a member of this Society from 1933 until 1963.

DAMN AND 'BLAST'! THE FRIENDSHIP OF WYNDHAM LEWIS AND AUGUSTUS JOHN

By MICHAEL HOLROYD, F.R.S.L.

(Read 30 November 1972)

Robert Gittings, C.B.E., Litt.D., F.R.S.L., in the Chair

THE long precarious friendship between Wyndham Lewis and Augustus John was unique in both their careers. Neither was an easy man; both had undeniable personalities; and in the course of their relationship they struck sparks off each other that light up peculiar corners of their characters.

John, who was four years older than Lewis, made his name far earlier. In 1898, the year that Lewis went up to the Slade School of Fine Art, John had left with honours thick upon him, in particular the Summer Composition Prize for his picture 'Moses and the Brazen Serpent'. Three years later he had already become something of a cult-figure among the students; and the walls of the Slade, Lewis recalled in *Rude Assignment*,

bore witness to the triumphs of this 'Michelangelo' . . . A large charcoal drawing in the centre of the wall of the life-class of a hairy male nude, arms defiantly folded and a bristling moustache, commemorated his powers with almost a Gascon assertiveness and fronting the stairs that led upwards where the ladies were learning to be Michelangelos, hung the big painting of Moses and the Brazen Serpent . . .

. . . One day the door of the life-class opened and a tall bearded figure with an enormous black Paris hat, large gold earrings decorating his ears, with a carriage of utmost arrogance strode in, and the whisper 'John' went round the class. He sat down on a donkey—the wooden chargers astride which we sat to draw—tore a page of banknote paper out of a sketch-book, pinned it upon a drawing board, and with a ferocious glare at the model (a female) began to draw with an indelible pencil. I joined the group behind this redoubtable personage. John left us as abruptly as he had arrived. We watched in silence this mythological figure depart.

It was about a year later that the two painters were formally introduced by William Rothenstein. Lewis by then was a good-looking, shy, gloweringly ambitious young man, who drew with thick black contours resembling the lead in a stained-glass window. He could be relied upon to act unpredictably, yet in the opinion of Professor Tonks who taught him at the Slade, he possessed the finest sense of line of any student there. Rothenstein took him to John's flat at 18 Fitzroy Street (which Lewis himself was later to occupy) probably in the summer of 1902: 'there was a noise of children,' Lewis afterwards recalled, 'for this patriarch had already started upon his Biblical courses'.

John had by now attracted a great deal of steam to himself, and for a time Lewis, made heady by this atmosphere, became his most formidable disciple. They stimulated and exasperated each other in about equal measures. Lewis was much impressed by all that John had so rapidly achieved. His success in art and with women appeared phenomenal, and by associating with him, Lewis seems to have felt, some of this success might rub off on him. John, on his side, was flattered by Lewis's veneration. Here was someone mysterious and remarkable, a poet hesitating between literature and painting, whose good opinion of him served to increase John's self-esteem. He seemed a valuable ally. Whatever else John felt, he was never bored by Lewis, whose dynamic progress through life was conducted as if to outwit some invisible foe. This involved a series of improbable retreats —to Scandinavia even, where he would find a letter from John asking: 'Tell me Lewis what of Denmark or—is Sweden safe?' Such places were not only safe, Lewis would hint in his replies, but the arenas of unimaginable conquests.

Very aware of his friend's superior education, John strove to match Lewis's 'calligraphic obscurity' by what he called 'linguistic licence'—a fantastic prolixity that he thought the intellectual tenor of their relationship demanded. The result was an exchange of letters, part undiscoverable, part indecipherable, covering over fifty years, that is almost complete in its comic density. Both were flamboyantly secretive men with bombardier tempers, and their friendship, which somehow endured all its volcanic quarrels, kept being arrested by declarations that it was at an end—an event upon which they would with great warmth congratulate themselves and each other. Yet such was the good feeling generated by these separations and congratulations that they quickly came together again when all the damning and blasting of their complicated liaison would start up once more.

Their correspondence, on both sides, is extremely generous with offensive advice which they attempt to make more palatable by adding at the end of the sentence the odd 'mon vieux' or 'old fellow'. John frequently intends to return Lewis's letters by post in order to get him, in the most friendly way of course, to 'admit [that] no more offensive statement could be penned'; but almost always he mislays the letter or, in his first fit of uncontrollable fury, flings it irrecoverably into some fire or sea. He is constantly being dumbfounded by Lewis's reminders to lend him money coupled with his forgetfulness in repaying it; and by his insistence that John was influencing mutual friends to his discredit. His style grows more and more convoluted in grappling with these groundless charges until it becomes blameless of almost all meaning. Then, suddenly, the clouds clear and in a succinct moment of retaliation he announces that Lewis's drawings 'lack *charm*, my dear fellow'.

The whole relationship is bedevilled by ingenious misunderstanding. Each credits the other with Machiavellian cunning, while assuming for himself a superhuman naïvety. Lewis is amazed that John never invites him for a drink; John is perplexed that Lewis is never able to visit him—when he does so, John is always out; while Lewis, on principle, never answers his doorbell. They make elaborate plans to meet on neutral territory, but then something goes wrong—the wrong time, the wrong place, the wrong mood. Lewis becomes increasingly irritated that John so seldom writes. John becomes irritated because, when he does write, his letters go astray, Lewis in the meantime having moved in darkest secrecy to some new unknown address—such as the Pall Mall Safe Deposit. The letters which do arrive express very adequately this irritation fanned, in Lewis's case, by eloquent invective and in John's by a circumlocution that marvellously avoids answering the most innocent of Lewis's inquiries. It is a most stimulating exchange.

Lewis's drawing of John, which is reproduced in *Blasting and Bombardiering*, is not among his best work; John's portraits of Lewis are. An early etching shows a handsome not ungentle face, though its moodiness is undisguised, and conveys the impression that John liked him, certainly thought him no fool. This etching and one other were done in January 1903; and a little later that year, at Matching Green in Essex, John painted an excellent oil portrait of Lewis, full of Castilian dignity displayed, as John Russell has observed, 'in a moment of repose'.

Lewis's description of John as a great 'man of action into whose hands the fairies put a brush instead of a sword'—a description which John himself was to define as rubbish—was a tribute to his physical personality. But on close companions the force of this personality was one of disintegration. In 1906, when the two of them were in Paris, Lewis wrote to his mother: 'I want to do some painting very badly, and can't do so near John . . . since his artistic personality is just too strong, and he is much more developed, naturally, and this frustrates any effort.' Partly because of this frustration, Lewis turned to his writing, being known by John as 'the Poet'. John respected Lewis's talent as an artist—in about 1910 he bought Lewis's *Porte de Mer*; and a little later Frank Rutter remembers John 'standing in admiration for fully twenty minutes before Wyndham Lewis's "Night Attack"'. But it was as a writer that he chiefly recommended him to others. Early in 1910 he is telling to the American lawyer John Quinn that 'my friend Lewis . . . is writing for the *English Review* and hopes to publish a book of poems in the autumn. I think he is certainly the most gifted of the young writers.' This veneration of Lewis's writings was genuine and lasted throughout his life. In 1930 he writes to him for publication:

In your 'Apes of God' you have, as it were, suspended upon magical wires colossal puppets, whose enlarged and distorted features may be attributed to those of not a few contemporary figures known to fame, infamy, and myself. Some of these you, from your own superabundance, have endowed with unexpected intelligence; others, by an ingenious operation of trepanning, you have bereft of what wits they had or could lay claim to. These grandiose toys you manipulate with a gargantuan and salutary art unexampled in our or in any other time I know of. Your readers and especially, I feel, your subjects, must be compelled, before the work of criticism begins, to salute with a wide and comprehensive flourish

the lofty genius of thea uthor. . . . This act of homage and surrender
I now myself perform.

Later still he praised very highly *The Childermass, Self-Condemned,*
and *The Revenge for Love.*

Lewis is equally full of public praise for John. It was John, he
writes, who 'inaugurated an era of imaginative art in England'.
Even in the 1940s and 1950s when John's powers were very
much in decline, Lewis always notices his paintings favourably;
and when John's autobiography *Chiaroscuro* appears, Lewis
reviews it well in *The Listener.* Such acts, which really belong to
the field of artistic trade unionism, seem to proclaim a friendship of enviable sweetness.

In fact they got on best when apart. During the years 1906
and 1907 when John was jostling between Paris and London,
and Lewis was on the move between England, France, and
Germany brewing up his Dostoievsky cocktail *Tarr,* they saw
a good deal of each other and their relationship rapidly over-
ripened. John's romantic admiration of his disciple now began
to evaporate, and what was left mingled curiously with lumps
of more indigestible emotion. They would go off to night-clubs
together, or sit drinking and talking in a café in the Rue
Dareau recommended by Sickert for its excellent *sauerkraut.*
'Not that I find him absolutely indispensible,' John conceded in
a letter to Alick Schepeler, 'but at times I love to talk with
him about Shelley or somebody.' Lewis himself, it seems,
preferred to talk of Apaches and 'to frighten young people'
with his tales of them. But what chiefly amused John was his
friend's odd and ineffectual love-affairs. These formed part of
his material for *Tarr* whose theme became sex and the artist,
displacing the stated one of its hero's spiritual progress. If the
male artist, Lewis seems to argue, finds much in his work that
other men seek of women, then it follows that he must be
particularly discriminating in his *affaires,* scrupulously avoid
sentimentality and all other false trails that lead him away
from reality. It was a theme nicely attuned to John's own
predicament, and almost certainly it formed part of their
regular conversations. John understood very well the conflict
between artistic integrity and appetite for life, knew that
overlapping territory between inspiration and gratification.
'I am like the noble, untaught and untainted savage who,
embracing with fearful enthusiasm the newly arrived Bottle,
Bible and Whore of civilization, contracts at once with
horrible violence their apoplectic corollary, the Paralysis, the

Hypocrisy and the Pox . . . So far I have been marvellously immune.'

Lewis's immunity, however, seemed far stronger. Prudence, suspicion and an aggressive shyness ringed him about like some fortress from which he seldom escaped. His *affaires* often appeared to be no more than word-affairs, though the words themselves were bold enough. 'Lewis announced last night that he was *loved*!' John reported to Alick Schepeler. 'At last! It seems he had observed a demoiselle in a restaurant who whenever he regarded her sucked in her cheeks slightly and looked embarrassed. The glorious fact was patent then—l'amour! He means to follow this up like a bloodhound. In the meanwhile, however, he has gone to Rouen for a week to see his mother, which in my opinion is not good generalship. He has a delightful notion— I am to get a set of young ladies during the summer as pupils and of course he will figure in the company and possibly be able to make love to one of them.' But when not in the vein to be amused by Lewis's eccentricities, John would quickly get needled. It was almost as if his own romanticism was being caricatured. 'The poet irritates me,' he admitted, 'he is always asking for petits suisses which are unheard of in this country and his prudence is boundless. What a mistake it is to have a friend—or, having one, ever to see him.'

In later years they made this mistake less often. But the romance of war drew them together again when, in the winter of 1917–18, they rather improbably found themselves occupying a large château near the Vimy front. Lewis appeared there as an ex-battery officer; John, to his evident confusion, as a Canadian Major. For both of them it was an untypically peaceful time—guns were everywhere, but for painting not firing. John, Lewis noticed with approval, did not neglect the social side of military life and was everywhere accorded the highest signs of respect, largely on account of his beard. 'He was the only officer in the British Army, excepting the King, who wore a beard', Lewis wrote. 'In consequence he was a constant source of anxiety and terror wherever he went. Catching sight of him coming down a road any ordinary private would display every sign of the liveliest consternation. He would start saluting a mile off. Augustus John—every inch a King George—would solemnly touch his hat and pass on.'

On one occasion, after a specially successful party, the two war-artists commandeered a car and careered off together almost into enemy lines. It was the closest John ever got to the fighting, and Lewis, the ex-bombardier, was soon poking fun at his friend's mock-war experiences. But John, observing that Lewis had quickly retreated home after their exploit, pursued him vicariously. 'Have you seen anything of that tragic hero and consumer of tarts and mutton-chops, Wyndham Lewis?' he asked a mutual girl-friend. 'He is, I think, in London, painting his gun-pit and striving to reduce his "Vorticism" to the level of Canadian intelligibility—a hopeless task I fear.'

A little later John was to join him back in London. Tiring of the stalemate of war, he had suddenly struck out, connecting with the chin of one of his allies, a notorious Canadian captain. A court martial was avoided by the intervention of Lord Beaverbrook, and John was hurried back to paint his war-picture, modestly entitled 'Fraternity', which now hangs in the Imperial War Museum.

Though Lewis was to blast many things, such as gipsydom, which John popularly represented, the clan John was safe. Augustus's son, Henry John, contributed to Lewis's paper *The Enemy*, and when he died in 1935 Lewis suggested 'some sort of book, assembling fragments perhaps of Henry's writing, to commemorate the promise of this young life'. Four years later, when Augustus's sister Gwen died, Lewis proposed bringing out a volume of her and Augustus's pictures and was only prevented by certain copyright difficulties from carrying this out.

Between the wars they corresponded tirelessly, made many secret plans for private meetings, but were not much connected in the public mind until, in 1938, they suddenly hit the head-lines together. It was this year that Lewis completed his famous portrait of T. S. Eliot—much admired by Eliot and by Lewis himself. In the spring it was submitted to the Royal Academy which, much to Eliot's relief and Lewis's indignation, rejected it. On learning this, John at once issued a statement, full of powerful negatives, for the press. 'I very much regret to make a sensation, but it cannot be helped', he began. 'Nothing that Mr. Wyndham Lewis paints is negligible or to be con-demned lightly. I strongly disagree with this rejection. I think it is an inept act on the part of the Academy. The rejection of Mr. Wyndham Lewis's portrait by the Academy has determined my decision to resign from that body . . . I shall henceforth experience no longer the uncomfortable feeling of being in a false position as a member of an institution with whose general policy I am constantly in disagreement. I shall be happier and

more honest in rejoining the ranks of those outside, where I
naturally belong.'

This statement provoked an extraordinary response in the
press in Britain, America, and, breaking through the walls of art
insularity, France. 'Premier May Be Questioned', ran a head-
line in the *Morning Post*. Elsewhere, with more bewilderment,
it was reported that the Academy itself had received no noti-
fication of John's resignation. In fact he had written a formal
letter to the President of the Royal Academy, Sir William
Llewelyn, three days beforehand, but had neglected to post it.
'After the crowning ineptitude of the rejection of Wyndham
Lewis's picture I feel it is impossible for me to remain any
longer a member of the R.A.', he told Llewelyn. Although in all
the press announcements John confessed to great 'reluctance' in
coming to his decision, he had in fact been searching round for
an avenue of escape from the Academy, partly because he
disliked Llewelyn. The Eliot portrait provided him with a
perfect motive, and he wrote to Lewis to thank him. 'I resign
with gratitude to you for affording me so good a reason.'

Lewis was delighted and suggested that all sorts of politico-
artistic activities should issue out of this rumpus, including the
formation by the two of them of a new *Salon des Refusés*. But
John demurred, 'being more than occupied with my show'.
This show, of John's Jamaican pictures, Lewis reviewed
enthusiastically in *The Listener*. 'As one passes in review these
blistered skins of young African belles, with their mournful
doglike orbs, and twisted lips like a heavyweight pugilist, one
comes nearer to the tragedy of this branch of the human race
than one would in pictures more literary in intention, such as
Gauguin would have supplied us with . . .

'Mr. John opens his large blue eyes, and a dusky head bursts
into them. He has his brushes and his canvas handy. His large
blue eyes hold fast the dusky object, while his brushes stamp
out on the canvas a replica of what he sees. But what he sees
(since he is a very imaginative man) is all the squalor and
beauty of the race—of this race of predestined underdogs who
have never been able to meet on equal terms the crafty white
man or the even more crafty Arab.

'In describing Mr. Augustus John's assault upon these Negro
belles—his optical assault, as his large blue eyes first fall upon
them in Jamaica—I was indicating what is, in fact, a good deal
of his method of work. Nature is for him like a tremendous
carnival, in the midst of which he finds himself. But there is

nothing of the spectator about Mr. John. He is very much part of
the saturnalia. And it is only because he enjoys it so tremendously
that he is moved to report upon it—in a fever of optical emotion,
before the object selected passes on and is lost in the crowd.'

In a letter to Lewis John thanked him for this article. 'It
does me a lot of good to have such a generous and understanding tribute from a man of your critical ability and I am
proud of it.' But he was not too proud to overlook the many
double entendres Lewis had used, and never for a moment lowered
his guard. Instead, he delivered a neatly placed blow just below
the belt when he let it be known that he had not seen the
portrait of Eliot at the time of its rejection, but that on doing
so later felt inclined to agree with the Academy. Two years
later, Llewelyn having left, he was re-elected to become what
Lewis described as 'the most distinguished Royal Academician
. . . of a sleeping-partner order'. To the end this jousting
between them continued. They conversed, for the most part,
by a series of back-handed compliments, of which perhaps the
finest is Lewis's 'I thank you quite unaffectedly for having
knocked a good deal of nonsense out of me, and am only sorry
that I was not able (owing to my tender years and extravagant
susceptibilities) to have rendered you a similar service'. Such
complimentary abuse, punctuated by sudden extraordinary
acts of kindness, seems to show a strange discrepancy between
their public and private exchanges. When Lewis went blind,
John boasted that he sent him a telegram expressing the hope
that it would not interfere with his real work: *art-criticism*.
And when pressed to explain this unsympathetic message, he
declared that he wasn't, through sentimentality, going to lay
himself open to some crushing rejoinder. In fact his letter was
not unsympathetic. 'I hope you will find a cure as did Aldous
Huxley,' he wrote. 'Anyhow indiscriminate vision is a curse.
Although without the aid of a couple of daughters like Milton,
I really don't see why you should discontinue your art criticism
—you can't go far wrong even if you do it in bed. You can
always turn on your private lamp of aggressive voltage along
with your dictaphone to discover fresh talent and demolish
stale.' At other times he treats this blindness as a gift of which
Lewis has taken full advantage. 'I have been *entranced* by this',
he writes to him of his novel *Rotting Hill* (10 December 1951),
'. . . and delighted to see that your present disability has in no
way impaired your powers of observation, but rather heightened
them.'

Lewis receives these 'impertinent' congratulations with an appreciative silence. He never once alluded to his blindness, preferring to make any accusation more obliquely: 'Dear John, I'm told you've mellowed.' John hotly denied the charge, but Tristan de Vere Cole remembers him taking Lewis out to dinner shortly before his death, seeing that his food was properly cut up, deferring to him in their conversation and exerting all his charm for Lewis's entertainment. At the end of John's essay on Lewis, 'Elephants with Beards', which appeared in his book *Finishing Touches* after both of them were dead, there is a gruff, almost grudging note of admiration for his old adversary: 'The heart which he had so successfully disciplined was now allowed to make its appearance at moments, though never vocally. Lewis was incapable of pathos, and practised to the end the reserve of a philosopher.'

In retrospect, the course of their friendship seems like an endless sparring match conducted in private so as to train them for real encounters against 'the Enemy'. For it was a common enemy they fought, and they go down fighting on the same side.

THE WEDMORE MEMORIAL LECTURE

This lecture perpetuates the memory of Sir Frederick Wedmore, author and critic. It was founded by his daughter, Millicent Wedmore, a member of this Society from 1928 until 1964.

HENRY JAMES AT HOME

By H. MONTGOMERY HYDE, M.A., D.LIT., F.R.HIST.S., F.R.S.L.

(Read 23 March 1972)

Robert Speaight, C.B.E., M.A., F.R.S.L., in the Chair.

THERE are several personal reasons why it gives me particular pleasure to have been asked to deliver this lecture. In the first place, Henry James was a relative of my mother's family in Ireland, our common ancestor William James having been a farmer in County Cavan. Secondly, I have been lucky enough to have lived in Henry James's English home—Lamb House, Rye—where he spent most of the last eighteen years of his life and where he wrote his later books. I had myself collected Henry James for years, I had read him—sometimes, I admit, with difficulty—and I had kept in touch with my James cousins on the other side of the Atlantic. But when I first visited Lamb House shortly after the end of the last war, I never thought that I would one day find myself living there. The house had been considerably damaged during an air raid in August 1940, and the attractive old Garden Room adjoining the house, where James used to write in summer, was almost completely destroyed, together with much of the library. In 1950, Lamb House was presented to the National Trust in accordance with the wish of the novelist's nephew, Henry James Junior of New York, who had inherited it under his uncle's will,—'to be preserved', in the words of the deed of gift, 'as an enduring symbol of the ties that unite the British and American people'.

I came to live in Lamb House in 1963 as the result of a paragraph which caught my eye in a London evening newspaper to the effect that the then tenants were leaving and that the National Trust was looking for someone to take over the tenancy. I applied to do so and after some delay—due to the fact that about a hundred other applicants had read the same newspaper report—I became the new tenant. My wife and I spent four very happy and rewarding years there, and we only left with considerable reluctance because of the ever mounting cost of the upkeep of the house and garden which, in the absence of any endowment accompanying the gift, fell (as it still does) entirely upon the tenant.

Finally, on a personal note, I am happy to think that Sir Frederick Wedmore, in whose memory the Wedmore Lecture was established by his daughter, and who was the art critic on *The Standard* for about thirty years, was originally appointed to this post by my great-grandfather James Johnstone, the newspaper's founder and first editor. How well James and Wedmore were acquainted I do not know, but I think they must have run across each other in London from time to time after James settled there in 1878; they must also surely have had a healthy respect for each other's work, based on a common love of France and French art and literature.

Henry James was a Fellow of this Society from 1907 until his death in 1916. He was elected a member of the Academic Committee in 1910 and two years later he became a Vice-President. Perhaps his most striking contribution to the Society's proceedings was the lecture he gave in 1912 on 'The Novel in *The Ring and the Book*' to commemorate the centenary of the birth of Robert Browning, whom he had known as a dining acquaintance for the last ten years of the poet's life and whose funeral he had attended in Westminster Abbey.

In public, James found Browning an idle gossip and thought he had a desire to monopolize the conversation with what he called 'a sort of shrill interruptingness' which showed 'a kind of vulgarity'. But Browning in his private life, as reflected by his writings, James regarded as a genius—'the writer of our time,' he described him, 'of whom, in the face of the rest of the world, the English tongue may be most proud—for he has touched everything, and with a breadth!' James especially singled out one quality in Browning's work which he admired. He called it 'the great constringent relation between man and woman at once at its maximum and as the relations most worth while for either party'. This remained, said James, the thing of which the poet's 'own rich experience most convincingly spoke of him.' Unfortunately James's own private life lacked

any such romantic episode with its dramatic overtones as that
between Robert Browning and Elizabeth Barrett. As a young
man, James had had an unhappy love affair, as he once hinted
to his friend Edmund Gosse, and although he had plenty of
women friends like Edith Wharton, Mrs. Humphrey Ward and
Violet Hunt, his relations with them were what is usually called
Platonic and he remained a bachelor to the end of his days.
For him the ideal relationship between a man and a woman
was personified in the Brownings—'never too much either of
the flesh or of the spirit . . . so long as the possibility of both of
these is in each, but always and ever as the thing absolutely
most worth while'. To the question he asked himself—was it
worth while for *them* or the reader?—James replied, 'Well, let
us say worth while assuredly for us in this noble exercise of the
imagination.'

Henry James was thirty-five years old when he settled in
London. Although born in New York, the family home was in
Cambridge near Boston, and there he was brought up and
lived with his parents, continuing to do so while he attended
the Harvard law school. The family were very comfortably off—
Henry's grandfather William, who was a younger son of the
farmer in Ireland, had emigrated to America about the time
of the War of Independence, his only belongings besides the
clothes he stood up in, so it is said, consisting of ten shillings and
a Latin grammar; he went into business in Albany, the New
York state capital, and when he died in 1832 was worth $2\frac{1}{2}$
million dollars. Thus Henry was able to travel extensively in
Europe, after leaving Harvard, with no financial worries,
eventually establishing himself in England which was to be his
home for the rest of his life.

His first accommodation was in London. It consisted of two
rooms, for which he paid two and a half guineas a week, on
the first floor of a Georgian house at the Piccadilly end of
Bolton Street. His sitting-room, where he ate and worked, had
a balcony from which he could catch a sideways glimpse of the
trees in Green Park.

The day after he installed himself in No. 3 Bolton Street,
Henry wrote to his sister Alice:

I have an excellent lodging in this excellent quarter, a lodging
whose dusky charms—including a housemaid with a prodigious
complexion but a demure expression and the voice of a duchess—
are too numerous to repeat. I have just risen from my first breakfast
of occasional tea, eggs, bacon and the exquisite English loaf, and

you may imagine the voluptuous glow in which such a repast has left me. *Chez moi* I am really well off—and it's a rare pleasure to feel warm in my room, as I sit scribbling, a pleasure I never knew in Paris. But after that charming city London seems almost superficially horrible, and general unaesthetic cachet. I am extremely glad, however, to have come here and feel completely that everything will improve on acquaintance.

The front door of the lodging was usually opened by a slender, tall, rather pretty girl, who was a relation of the landlady. 'She's an English character', Henry remarked to an American friend when he got to know her. 'She's what they call in England a "person". She isn't a lady and she isn't a woman; she's a person.' One thing about her Henry always remembered. The smallest witticisim on his part produced uncontrollable fits of laughing. 'Oh please don't, Mr James!' she would giggle. 'It's quite too funny!'

Then there was Louisa, the dark-faced maid with the ducal voice, who brought him his first breakfast. She would also bring him other meals if he needed them, but these usually consisted of a chop and boiled potatoes. The maid helped in the kitchen, and once, without apparent success, Henry tried to get her to introduce a little variety into the cooking of the potatoes. He described the conversation in a letter to his sister Alice:

H. J. (to the maid): Can't you do anything in the world with potatoes but drearily boil them?
The Maid: Oh dear yes, sir, certainly, we can *mash* them!
H. J. That comes to the same thing. No other way?
The Maid: I don't think we have heard of any other way, sir.
H. J. You can't fry them?
The Maid: I don't think we could do that, sir? Isn't that French cookery sir?

Eventually the maid left to marry a deformed cobbler, whose acquaintance she had made in the neighbourhood. When her successor arrived, Henry asked her what her name was.

Well, sir, it might be Maria.
It *might* be? Henry queried in surprise.
Well, sir, they calls me Maria, the newcomer admitted.
Isn't it your name?
My name's Annie, sir, but Missus says that's too familiar.

So Henry 'compromised' and called her Annie-Maria. 'It is part of the British code that you can call a servant any name you like,' he explained for the benefit of the family in Cambridge, 'and many people have a fixed name for their butler, which all the successive occupants of the place are obliged to assume, so that the family needn't change its habits.'

The house in Bolton Street was pulled down some years ago, but the three other buildings where he lived in London are still extant—first, the flat he occupied on the fourth floor of 34 De Vere Gardens in Kensington from 1885 to 1896, 'my chaste and secluded Kensington *quatrième*', he called it. Later, there was the Reform Club where he kept a room; and finally another flat, at 21 Carlyle Mansions in Cheyne Walk, Chelsea, with its view of the river which he took in 1913 and where he died three years later.

After moving in to De Vere Gardens, he wrote: 'My flat is perfection and ministers more than I can say to my health, to my spirits and my work.'

He engaged a married couple called Smith as servants on living-in board wages of £10 a month, the man as butler-valet and the wife as cook. Mrs. Smith was a rather frightened looking creature, who would interview the master every morning, in a large white apron, to get her 'orders for the day'. Unfortunately, Smith developed into a heavy drinker and eventually had to be got rid of. Henry regarded him as 'an excellent fellow', at least in the early days, although the butler's intellectual qualities do not seem to have been particularly brilliant. 'When I give him an order,' Henry told his friend Edith Wharton, 'he had to go through three successive mental processes before he could understand what I was saying. First he had to register the fact that he was being spoken to, then to assimilate the meaning of the order given him, and lastly to think out what practical consequences might be expected to follow if he obeyed it.' On the other hand, as Mrs. Wharton dryly observed, perhaps these mental gymnastics were excusable in the circumstances.

As he grew older, Henry felt more and more the need for intellectual companionship: 'Could you by a miracle,' he wrote to Edmund Gosse, shortly after he had established himself in De Vere Mansions, 'if you are not afraid of a very modest dinner, come and break bread with me tonight at the primitive hour of seven? I am alone, and there is a solitary fowl. But she shall be dressed with intellectual sauce . . . I am famished for a little literary conversation. In this city of 5,000,000 souls, but not, alas, brains, I find *none*.'

It was the shocking failure of Henry James's play *Guy Domville* at the old St. James's Theatre in 1895, when the author and the actor-manager George Alexander were both hissed off the stage as they took a curtain at the end of the performance on the first night, that largely determined James to abandon the theatre and to look for a place in the country where he could spend the greater part of the year, henceforth concentrating on his novels and short stories. He got possession of Lamb House by a lucky chance, as indeed I myself was to do nearly seventy years later. One day, towards the end of 1895, he called on an architect friend, Edward Warren, in Westminster, and saw a coloured sketch of the Garden Room which Warren had made on a recent visit to Rye. This caught his fancy. The following summer James was lent a cottage near Rye and one afternoon he walked over to see what he called 'the mansion with the garden house perched on the wall'. He promptly lost his heart to the place; but on making some inquiries in the town he was disappointed to learn that the house was already occupied, and that there seemed no likelihood of its becoming vacant, for when the elderly owner died, so he was told, it was certain to pass into the hands of his son.

How the unexpected came about just over a year later is described by Henry James in a letter he wrote at the time to Alice James, his brother William's wife:

There was no appearance whatever that one could ever have it; either that its fond proprietor would give it up or that if he did it could come at all within one's means: So I simply sighed and renounced; tried to think no more about it, till at last, out of the blue, a note from the good local ironmonger, to whom I had whispered at the time my hopeless passion, informed me that by the sudden death of the owner and the preference (literal) of his son for Klondike it might perhaps drop into my lap. Well, to make a long story short, it *did* immediately drop and more miraculous still to say, on terms, for a long lease, well within one's means—terms quite deliciously moderate.

And so James became the tenant of the house with its delightful walled garden which had been built by James Lamb, a former Mayor of Rye, early in the eighteenth century. He signed the lease at a rent of £70 a year—this 'most portentious parchment', as he called it, now hangs in the hall at Lamb House. Two years later the excitement of the Klondike gold rush proved too much for the landlord who died, and James was able to buy the freehold for £2,000. For this very reasonable sum he got a fine oak-panelled residence with over a dozen rooms, a brick-built studio on the other side of the garden, besides the Garden Room and the right to use a private pew in Rye Parish Church.

When he moved into Lamb House, in the spring of 1898, James was fifty-five years of age, an expatriate American with an established literary reputation on both sides of the Atlantic. The first of his books to be written in Lamb House was *The Awkward Age*, and the house admittedly served as the model for Mr. Longdon's in that novel. The ghost story 'The Third Person', which first appeared in the collection of short stories published under the title *The Soft Side* in 1900, also had Lamb House for its setting. Other novels written in the house included *The Wings of the Dove*, *The Ambassadors* and *The Golden Bowl*, as well as a number of essays, plays and travel books. He also planned and produced the New York edition of his collected *Novels and Tales* with their elaborate Prefaces.

Living was cheap in those days; and, although James never made very much money in the way of royalties from his later writings, he had a small income of his own. Besides a private secretary, who lived in the town, he kept an indoor domestic staff of four—a married couple who served as butler and cook, a parlourmaid and a housemaid. Fairly early on in James's occupation of Lamb House, the married couple who had been dismissed due to the husband's overfondness for alcohol were replaced by a cook-housekeeper, named Mrs. Paddington— 'a pearl of price' James called her—and a houseboy, Burgess Noakes, who helped the parlourmaid to wait at table. Noakes later graduated from houseboy to butler-cum-valet and was to nurse James in his last years of ill-health with touching devotion. There was also a gardener named George Gammon; 'an excellent, quiet, trustworthy fellow in all respects', was how his master described him.

Several guests who enjoyed the Master's hospitality at Lamb House have recorded their memories of the host in residence. One of them was Arthur Christopher Benson, then a schoolmaster at Eton and afterwards Master of Magdalene College, Cambridge. He described his visit in his diary:

Lamb House, Rye, January 17, 1900 . . . Henry James, looking somewhat cold, tired and old, met me at the station: most affectionate, patting me on the shoulder and really welcoming, with abundance of *petits soins* . . .

We walked slowly up and came to Lamb House. It is sober red

Georgian; facing you as you come up is the bow-window of the Garden House with all its white casements—used by H. J. to write in in summer. The house has a tall door, strangely fortified inside by bolts, admitting into a white panelled hall. There are three small panelled sitting rooms, besides the dining room. The place has been carefully done up, and is very clean, trim, precise, but all old and harmonious . . .

Dined simply at 7.30 with many apologies from H. J. about the fare . . . He was full of talk, though he looked weary, often passing his hand over his eyes; but he was refined and defined, was intricate, magniloquent, rhetorical, humorous, not so much like a talker, but like a writer repeating his technical processes aloud—like a savant working out a problem.

H. J. works hard; he establishes me in a little high-walled white parlour, very comfortable, but is full of fear that I am unhappy. He comes in, pokes the fire, presses a cigarette on me, puts his hand on my shoulder, looks inquiringly at me, and hurries away. His eyes are *piercing*. To see him, when I came down to breakfast this morning, in a kind of Holbein square cap of velvet and black velvet coat, scattering bread on the frozen lawn to the birds, was delightful . . .

We lunched together with his secretary, a young Scot. H. J. ate little, rolled his eyes, waited on us, walked about, talked—finally hurried me off for a stroll before my train. All his instincts are of a kind that make me feel vulgar—his consideration, hospitality, care of arrangement, thoughtfulness. . . . We got to the station; he said an affectionate farewell, pressing me to come again; I went away refreshed, stimulated, sobered, and journeyed under a dark and stormy sky to the dreary and loathsome town of Hastings.

By the time he took up his abode in Lamb House, Henry James had acquired the habit of dictating his compositions to a secretary or amanuensis. This was done straight on to the typewriter, which tended to increase the prolixity of his literary style, as evidenced by most of his compositions at this period. His friend and fellow novelist E. F. Benson has recalled a June day around the turn of the century when he was staying in the house and heard the voice of 'the Master' from within the Garden Room dictating to his typist the novel on which he was engaged.

It boomed out through the open window between the tassels of wisteria, now louder, now softer, as he paced up and down the length of the room, and the metallic click of the typewriter made response. From breakfast until the stroke of the gong for lunch he was thus invisible though not inaudible: then there came a day when, though the morning was still only half-spent, he emerged from the inviolable precinct, and taking me by the arm he walked me about the lawn, and involved himself in a noble harangue. To me, he said, fresh from the roar and reverberation of London with its multifarious movements and intensive interests, the news he was about to impart might reasonably seem to be of little moment, but to him in his quiet and red walled *angulus terrae*, this little plot in Rye, that which had in fact happened this morning, and which was the cause of his indulging himself now with a mulberry at this unusual hour . . .

On and on went the magnificent architectural period, and then, I suppose, not having the typist to read it out to him and thus give him a clue through the labrynth, he confessed himself lost, and added, 'In fact, my dear Fred Benson, I have finished my book . . .'

Another guest was his fellow countrywoman and novelist Edith Wharton; apart from his brother William she was probably his closest personal and literary friend—'the Angel of Devastation', he used to call her. 'Some of my richest hours were spent under his roof', she has recalled.

From the moment when I turned the corner of the grassgrown street mounting steeply between squat brick houses, and caught sight at its upper end of the wide Palladian window of the garden-room a sense of joyous liberation bore on me. There *he* stood on the doorstep, the white-panelled hall with its old prints and crowded bookcases forming a background to his heavy loosely-clad figure. Arms outstretched, lips and eyes twinkling, he came down to the car uttering cries of mock amazement and mock humility at the undeserved honour of my visit. The arrival at Lamb House was an almost ritual performance, from those first ejaculations to the large hug and the two solemn kisses executed in the middle of the hall rug. Then, arm in arm, through the oak-panelled morning-room we wandered out on to the thin worn turf of the garden, with its ancient mulberry tree, its unkempt flower-borders, the gables of Watchbell Street peeping like village gossips over the creeper-clad walls and the scent of roses spiced with a strong smell of the sea. Up and down the lawn we strolled with many pauses, exchanging news, answering each other's questions, delivering messages from other members of the group, inspecting the strawberries and lettuces in the tiny kitchen-garden and the chrysanthemums 'coming along' in pots in the greenhouse; till at length the parlour-maid appeared with a tea-tray and I was led up the rickety outside steps into the garden-room, that stately and unexpected appendage to the unadorned cube of the house . . .

Edith Wharton regarded herself as a literary disciple of Henry's, being like him concerned with artistic form in her novels and looking to moral values behind the upper-class social scene of which she wrote. But it was a case of the disciple outstripping the Master, certainly from the point of view of the commercial success of her books, which sold far better than his. That he was painfully aware of the difference may be gathered from Henry's reaction to a remark she made one day when they were driving together near Rye in her large new limousine. The magnificent vehicle had, she said, been bought with the proceeds of her last novel. 'With the proceeds of *my* last novel,' said Henry with wry irony, 'I purchased a small go-cart, or hand-barrow, on which my guests' luggage is wheeled from the station to my house. It needs a coat of paint. With the proceeds of my next novel, I shall have it painted.'

James's manservant Burgess Noakes has described his master's daily round:

> I used to call him every morning regular at eight o'clock [Mr. Noakes told me]. After that he'd have his breakfast. He'd come down about nine o'clock, and about ten o'clock he would start work with his secretary. He was very regular in his habits, he'd work on till about one o'clock. . . . He'd have his lunch, and after lunch, he'd take his walk. He was a stout heavily built man, but he was very active, right up to the last, too. Off he'd go with his little dog, and many a time I watched him out of the door. Before he got half way up the street towards the church you'd see him stop, the stick would go down—there he'd stand, with his head slightly bent and his finger in his watch-chain, and all of a sudden he'd go again. He had a habit—if he wanted to remember anything or remind himself of anything—he had a habit of trying a knot in his watch-chain, sometimes two.

According to his servant, the Master objected to the use of coal gas except in the kitchen, preferring oil lamps to illuminate the living rooms. The lamps frequently smoked and the Master would often fall asleep late at night, after his secretary had left, to be awakened by the faithful Burgess, his face covered with lamp black.

James's first woman secretary, Miss Mary Weld, later Mrs. Kingdon, found him kind and considerate to work for. He discovered she liked flowers, and he would pick a small bunch from the garden each morning and put them beside her typewriter. He would also give her useful advice. One day walking with her down the steep hill of Mermaid Street, they passed a short-haired girl wearing a stiff collar and tie. 'That young girl is the epitome of everything that a woman should not look like', he exclaimed. 'Glory in your femininity, Miss Weld!'

Poor Miss Weld was painfully conscious that her sailor hat was rather like the one the girl was wearing. As soon as they parted, Miss Weld went off and bought a hat with mignonette on it. Next day when she wore it he didn't say a word. He did, however, smile his approval.

According to Miss Weld, he always treated women with reverence; nothing distressed him more than a woman trying to look like a man. Once when his niece Peggy (later Mrs. Bruce Porter) came to stay, bringing with her some hockey sticks, James was horrified by the sight. 'Miss Weld,' he said, 'take her out this afternoon and teach her something feminine.'

Miss Weld was succeeded at the typewriter by Miss Theodora Bosanquet. She evidently preferred chocolates to flowers as a literary stimulus, and James would place several bars beside her Remington machine after peeling off the silver paper. He had begun the practice of dictating his novels in the nineties, and by 1907, the year Miss Bosanquet came to work for him, this had become a confirmed habit. Its effects were easily recognizable in his style, which seemed to his secretary to become more and more like free involved unanswered talk. He once said to her, 'I know I am too diffuse when I am dictating.' At the same time he felt that the gain in expression through the use of what he laughingly called 'Remingtonese' more than compensated for any loss of concision. He had now reached the stage at which, as Miss Bosanquet put it, 'the click of the Remington acted as a positive spur'. According to her, he found it virtually impossible to compose to the music of any other make. During one fortnight when the Remington was out of order, he dictated to an Oliver with evident discomfort; he found it almost impossibly disconcerting to speak to something which made no responsive sound at all. Once or twice, when he was ill in bed, his secretary would take down a note or two in shorthand, but as a rule he insisted on the Remington being moved into his bedroom for even the shortest letters.

Miss Bosanquet recalled his absentmindedness, how he would sometimes invite people to lunch and then forget all about them. One day about one o'clock, when he was still dictating, there was a knock on the front door. He tiptoed to the window and looked out cautiously. 'Motor people', he said. 'Two of them, done up in goggles.' Then, suddenly, he remembered: 'Oh, good Lord!' he said. 'They have come to lunch. I asked them. I must go and see Mrs Paddington at once. Oh, why can't people keep away!' A few minutes later, he came back and explained that they were honeymooners from Brighton. The bride had written to him and he had put her letter in a conspicuous place, and had then forgotten all about it. Theodora Bosanquet expressed the hope that Mrs. Paddington had risen to the occasion. 'Oh, yes', he said. 'She did. She drew out of the oven a fillet of beef which she had been cooking for herself. 'Give that to me,' I cried. And then, he went on, 'What an infernal nuisance it all is. Motor cars are the curse of the age. Before their day no one would have dreamt of coming over from Brighton.'

In the winter months James used to work in the Green Room on the first floor, so named (as it still is) from the colour of its panelling. 'It had many advantages as a winter workroom,' Miss Bosanquet has recalled, 'for it was small enough to be easily warmed and a wide south window caught all the morning sunshine. . . . It never failed to give the owner pleasure to look out of this convenient window at his English garden where he could watch his English gardener digging the flowerbeds or mowing the lawn or sweeping up fallen leaves. . . . Three high bookcases, two big writing desks and an easy chair filled most of the space in the Green Room but left enough clear floor for a restricted amount of the pacing exercise that was indispensable to literary composition.'

For two years, from 1907 to 1909, James worked with Miss Bosanquet on the Collected Edition of his *Novels and Tales*, usually known as the New York edition, which appeared in twenty-four volumes under the imprint of Scribner's in New York and Macmillan in London. Each volume contained a frontispiece photogravure by Alvin Langdon Coburn, a brilliant and original young American photographer, whose work had first been exhibited in London in 1900 when the photographer was only eighteen. Having effectively photographed, among others, Bernard Shaw, George Meredith, H. G. Wells and G. K. Chesterton in England, Coburn returned to America in 1905 to do a series of photographic portraits of American authors for the *Century Magazine*. The authors included Henry James, who happened to be on a visit to the United States in that year and was duly photographed in Coburn's New York studio. The two men were instantly drawn to each other. 'There are some people you cannot help liking the moment you see them,' Coburn said afterwards, 'and Henry James was, for me, such a person.' For his part, James invited the young man to come down for a night to Lamb House where he was then living, as soon as they both were back in

England. He explained that he wanted a photograph of himself as the frontispiece to the first volume of the forthcoming collected edition of his *Novels and Tales*. James was so pleased with the result that he asked the young photographer to take pictures for use in other volumes, which Coburn willingly agreed to do. He proposed that together they should hunt for what he called 'a series of reproducible subjects . . . of images always confessing themselves mere optical symbols or echoes, expressions of no particular thing in the text, but only the type of idea of this or that thing . . . at the most pictures of our "set" stage with the actors left out'. So, after photographing the outside of Lamb House for *The Awkward Age*, Coburn was despatched first to Paris and then to Venice and Rome in search of more 'reproducible subjects'.

Henry's instructions were thorough and 'young Alvin', as the Master came to call him, was amazed by his detailed knowledge of the Paris streets. The photographer was first directed to search for a gateway to an old 'aristocratic' house. The instructions continued:

There are even possibly three or four such *portes-cochères* on the quays of the Left Bank. . . . But look for a grand specimen of the type, as I told you, at the British Embassy, in the Rue Faubourg St. Honoré. . . . And there are two or three others, very nearly as majestic, in the same street: only these are too modern, and also *too* majestic. But I repeat for you that, once you get the Type into your head, you will easily recognise specimens by walking about in the *old* residential and 'noble' parts of the city: by which I mean particularly the Faubourg St. Germain. (Not but that there are plenty of featureless houses too.) Tell the cabman that you want to drive through every street in it, and then, having got that notion, go back and walk and stare at your ease . . .

After making further detailed suggestions as to what the photographer should look for, particularly on the Left Bank, James concluded:

These are the principal things I think of; though if you could rake in one or two big generalizing glimpses of fragments (even of the Arc de Triomphe, say), there are one or two other places—as the second volume of *Princess Casamassima*—where suchlike might come in.
My blessing on your inspiration and your weather!

During this visit inspiration and weather combined to produce seven excellent pictures, which were used for the New York edition. They were a typical house in the Faubourg

St. Germain, which appeared as the frontispiece to *The American*; the Arc de Triomphe behind the trees in the Champs Elysées (entitled 'Splendid Paris, Charming Paris') for the second volume of *Princess Casamassima*; the Comédie Française with its colonnade for the first volume of *The Tragic Muse*; the 'Court of the Hotel' (actually the Hotel St. James in the Rue Faubourg St. Honoré where Coburn stayed) for *The Reverberators*; and finally 'By Notre Dame' and 'The Luxembourg Garden' for the two volumes of *The Ambassadors*.

In his autobiography Coburn has recalled his next meeting with his collaborator:

Early in November [1906] Henry James came up to London and we gloated together over my prints. Though sixty-three years old, H. J. was like a boy, always displaying unquenchable and contagious enthusiasm for every detail concerning these illustrations. This made it a joy to work with him. That is the splendid thing about an artist, whether his medium of expression be pigments, or sounds, or words, or even the Art of Life, he does not 'grow up', grow stale, or lose freshness of outlook; and Henry James was a true artist in this respect. He never lost the capacity to see things with that freshness of vision, as they are beheld by the very young or the very wise.

The photographer's Italian pilgrimage yielded four subjects, two in Rome and two in Venice. The Roman pictures were 'The Roman Bridge' (in fact the Ponte Sant'Angelo surmounted by Bernini's colossal statues of angels) for the second volume of *Portrait of a Lady*, and 'By St. Peter's' for *Daisy Miller*. The two pictures of Venice, 'Juliana's Court' and 'The Venetian Palace', were to form the frontispieces respectively to *The Aspern Papers* and the second volume of *The Wings of the Dove*.

Before Coburn set off for Italy, James had written to him: 'Make your mother dress you warmly for the journey to Venice, which I think (I am in fact sure) you will, with the elasticity of youth, really enjoy.' Coburn arrived in Venice in the middle of December, but his enjoyment was tempered by the climate which he did not expect. 'Never before or since have I felt so miserably cold or damp,' he afterwards recalled,—'until I moved into a German pension with enormous stoves and old-fashioned feather beds.'

'Juliana's Court' was the actual place James had in mind when writing *The Aspern Papers*. However, the original Juliana had lived in old age in Florence, where she died. She was Claire Clairmont, Byron's mistress and mother of their daughter

Allegra, and the Aspern papers of the novel were in fact those of Shelley. The building which James took for his setting was the Casa Capello in the Rio Marin, then occupied by an elderly lady, Mrs. Fletcher, and her literary daughter Constance who wrote novels under the pseudonym of 'George Fleming' and whom James warned of the photographer's impending arrival.

I have told her exactly what I want you to do, outside and in, [he wrote to Coburn on the eve of his departure] and as she is a very kind and artistic person, you can trust yourself completely to her for guidance. She will expect you, and will, I am sure, respond to my request on your behalf in a cordial and sympathetic spirit. Your best way to get to Rio Marin will be to obtain guidance, for a few coppers, from some alert Venetian street-boy (or of course you can go romantically in a gondola). But the extremely tortuous and complicated walk will show you so much, so many bits and odds and ends, such a revel of Venetian picturesqueness, that I advise you doing it on foot as much as possible.

Then, after giving young Alvin further directions as to how to find the Casa Capello by taking a vaporetto to the railway station and walking from there, he went on:

For the other picture, that for *The Wings of the Dove*, I had vaguely in mind the Palazzo Barbaro, which you can see very well from the first, the upper, of the iron bridges, the one nearest the mouth of the Grand Canal, and which crosses from Campo San Stefano to the great Museum of the Academy. The Palace is the very old Gothic one, on your right, just before you come to the iron bridge, after leaving (on the vaporetto) the steam-boat station of the Piazza. . . . But I don't propose you should attempt here anything but the outside; and you must judge best if you can rake the object most effectively from the bridge itself, from the little campo in front of the Academy, from some other like spot further—that is further towards the Salute, or from a gondola (if your gondolier can keep it steady enough) out on the bosom of the Canal . . .

And do any other odd and interesting bit you can, that may serve for a sort of symbolised and generalised Venice in case everything else fails; preferring the noble and fine aspect, however, to the merely shabby and familiar (as in the case of those views you already have)—yet especially *not* choosing the pompous and obvious things that one everywhere sees photos of.

In the event Coburn succeeded in taking an excellent photograph of the Palazzo Barbaro, a building of operatic as well as architectural interest, for 'La Donna' of the celebrated aria 'La Donna è Mobile' in Verdi's *Rigoletto* lived there in fact, just as James's fictitious heroine Milly Theale did in the author's imagination.

The next images were to be in London. As the frontispiece to *The Spoils of Poynton* James secured permission from the Keeper of the Wallace Collection for Coburn to photograph some of the furnishings in Gallery 21. This room had formerly been Sir Richard Wallace's study and contained a particularly fine chimney piece. As usual James's directions were delightfully explicit:

And take the beautiful subject *obliquely*, won't you?—and with as much of the damask on the wall as possible. And, further, please give the attendant, as a tip, 2/6 from me; (I will send you a postal order in the morning—I can't buy one today Sunday.) I also enclose my own card.

The result which James entitled 'Some of the Spoils' shows how well the photographer carried out his instructions. Other pictures were obtained in the course of expeditions or 'prowls' as James called them which they took together. 'Henry James knew his London as few men have known it, in all its quaintness, its mystery, and its charm,' Coburn was to recall sixty years later. 'He obviously enjoyed our search.'

The afternoon that we went to St. John's Wood [wrote Alvin Coburn in his autobiography] to photograph the little gateway and house which was to serve as the illustration for the second volume of *The Tragic Muse* was an unforgettable experience. It was a lovely afternoon, I remember, and H. J. was in his most festive mood. I was carefree because this time I did not have to hunt for the subject, for I had the most perfect and dependable guide, the creator and author himself. I had not even read *The Tragic Muse*, but I shared his enthusiasm when after considerable searching we came on exactly the right subject. Where the house was located, I do not now recall, it may in fact no longer exist, for so much of London has passed away into the domain of forgotten things; but in the photograph it is preserved, crystallised as a memento of what Henry James had meant it to be.

Now it was tea-time, and pleasantly fatigued by our exertions, now triumphantly rewarded, we looked for a teashop to refresh ourselves, but were only able to find a baker's shop. We descended on this and came out with Bath buns, which we thankfully devoured as we walked down the street.

The incident of the Bath buns also remained in James's memory and he invariably used to recall it with a chuckle. On another occasion they went in a hansom cab to Hampstead in the rain to photograph the seat on which James and his friend, the artist, George Du Maurier, had so often sat, and James left his fine silver-headed walking stick with the driver as assurance of their return when they left him on the edge of the Heath. (The stick, by the way, is now in my possession.) Other London jaunts yielded 'The Cage', a view of a post office-cum-general store for *In the Cage*—with best tea and coffee shown as selling for 1*s*. 4*d*. a pound—'The Doctor's Door', recognizable as 143 Harley Street, for the first volume of *The Wings of the Dove*, and 'The Curiosity Shop' for the first volume of *The Golden Bowl*. For the second volume of *The Golden Bowl*, which was to be the last in the series, apart from the two supplementary volumes which came out after James's death, the novelist felt, as he put it, that 'nothing would so nobly serve as some generalized vision of Portland Place,' when 'at a given moment the great Philistine vista would itself perform a miracle, would become interesting for a splendid atmospheric hour, as only London knows how, and that our business would be to understand'. Indeed 'the great Philistine vista' of Portland Place inspired one of Coburn's happiest efforts, with its setting of a hansom cab on a foggy winter's afternoon. It was to become one of the photographer's favourite pictures, and he used it for the jacket of his autobiography which was published in 1966. My regret is that these pictures are not included in the various later editions of James's collected works.

One final picture of Henry James at home—this time in his flat in Cheyne Walk, where Compton Mackenzie went to call on him in the spring of 1914. As a boy, twenty-three years earlier, Mackenzie had been taken to see the Master in De Vere Gardens by his father, the actor-manager Edward Compton, to discuss the production of the dramatized version of James's novel *The American*, in which Compton played the title role. Now, early in 1914, James had written an article for the *Times Literary Supplement* in which the Master had put Compton Mackenzie on the same level as another rising young novelist Hugh Walpole, which drew a protest from Mackenzie. According to him, the Master held up his hands in a great gesture of consternation and said to him, gasping for the words he wanted as if they were moths fluttering round him, 'You, you amaze me, you, you astound me. All I thought I'd said about our excellent, our dear young friend Hugh Walpole was that up to the present moment he had written absolutely nothing!'

'And now,' Henry continued, 'I want to hear all about your work.' Just as he said this, his housekeeper came in with the news that a man from the Army and Navy Stores had arrived, and would Mr. James send an order for some marmalade?

The rising young novelist was at a loss to understand why the housekeeper could not give the order herself, but apparently Henry had to give it in writing.

'Forgive me, my dear, my dear young friend this appalling intrusion from the great outside world, and . . .' he turned towards the housekeeper—'marmalade, did you say, Mrs Anderson?'

'Marmalade, Mr. James.'

'Well what will engage you for a moment, my dear boy, while I go into this complicated question?' He picked up two books from the table. 'Now here's our dear H. G.'s last book', he went on. 'I wasn't quite sure whether our dear H. G.—or here's our dear Arnold Bennett's last book—perhaps you'd like to turn the pages of that or . . .'

'Mr James, the man is waiting.'

'Aha, ah yes—yes, yes!'

Henry thereupon sat down at the table, took a pen and dipped it in the ink and held it poised over the paper. 'Marmalade', he murmured to himself. 'How, how should one address the directors of this vast emporium—this huge agglomeration—on marmalade?'

'Six jars, Mr. James,' said the housekeeper, who had noticed the Master's hesitation.

'Please, Mrs. Anderson, I must give attention to this. It's not one of those—um—' At this, he broke off and turned again to his young visitor. 'Are you sure, my dear boy? If you don't find that book, dear H. G.'s, interesting or Arnold Bennett's, there's another here by—'

'Mr. James, Mr. James,' the housekeeper beseeched him. 'Please, the man is waiting.'

'Ah, marmalade!'

According to Mackenzie, this performance went on without exaggeration for quite five minutes before Henry got down to ordering from the Army and Navy Stores six two-pound pots of Oxford marmalade, eventually dismissing his housekeeper with a characteristic lament for 'these co-operative stores which our Frankenstein of a civilization has created to destroy the amenity of existence'.

Henry James died in his London flat on 28 February 1916.

George Gammon, the gardener at Lamb House, who came up for the funeral in Chelsea Old Church, was asked by Mrs. Alice James, Henry's sister-in-law—his brother William's widow—who was in charge of the arrangements if he would like to take a last look at his dead master. As he was doing so, Mrs. James remarked that he looked at peace. 'Yes, ma'am,' said the gardener, 'he's kept very well, hasn't he?' Her comment in telling this story afterwards was, 'How Henry would have loved to hear him!'

I doubt whether Henry James ever considered himself a suitable subject for a formal biography, although Professor Leon Edel after devoting more than twenty years to the project had just produced his fifth and final volume. During one of his last visits to Lamb House, James made a great bonfire in the garden of all the letters addressed to him and other papers which he had kept. It was known that there was a secret drawer in his desk; but if his nephew and heir expected this to yield some unpublished literary treasure, he was disappointed. When the drawer was opened, all it contained were two medical prescriptions, one for reading-spectacles and the other for gout, a particularly potent remedy which the local chemist used to make up. The gout prescription, by the way, is preserved in the house with the desk and other relics of the Master, including a small portion of his library which survived the bombing in 1940.

The year before he died, Henry James became a British subject as a gesture of sympathy for Britain in the First World War. Four sponsors were necessary to vouch formally for his eligibility for British citizenship. On being approached to act as one of them, the Prime Minister, Mr. Asquith, said he would be delighted, although he added afterwards in a jocular aside that 'the bonds of friendship were stretched to cracking point when I had to subscribe the proposition that he could both talk and write English'. The Home Secretary, Sir John Simon, obligingly expedited the application and issued the certificate of naturalization within a few days of receiving the papers. On 26 July 1915 Henry James became a citizen of the United Kingdom of Great Britain and Ireland. Next day he took the Oath of Allegiance before a Commissioner in his lawyer's office. 'The odd thing is that I don't feel a bit different', he told Edmund Gosse, another of his sponsors. 'The process has only shown me what I virtually *was* . . .'

In October 1915 he had paid his last visit to Lamb House, 'for whose garden and old battered purple wall', he once said, he would 'give the whole bristling state of Connecticut'. He asked to be taken back there during his final illness. It was not possible to move him; but he made the journey in his imagination, since he spoke to Burgess Noakes of his pleasure at being back. In the New Year's Honours in 1916 he was awarded the Order of Merit, and the insignia of this high mark of royal favour was brought to him on his death-bed. On the headstone of his grave in the family burial ground in Cambridge, Massachusetts, he is described simply but truly as 'novelist and interpreter of his generation on both sides of the sea'. As a near kinsman who has been privileged to live in the house he loved so well, and as a Fellow of the Society of which he was such a distinguished ornament, I salute his memory this evening.

GIFF EDMONDS MEMORIAL LECTURE

This lecture perpetuates the memory of Lieutenant
Nicholas Gifford Edmonds, of the 2nd Black Watch,
who was killed at Magersfontein on 11 December
1899. It was founded by his sister, Sophie Edmonds,
a member of this Society from 1919 to 1945.

FRANCIS KILVERT AND HIS DIARY

By WILLIAM PLOMER, C.B.E., D.LITT., F.R.S.L.

(*Read 19 July 1972*)

Lord Butler, K.G., C.H., President R.S.L., in the Chair

THIRTY-FIVE years ago nobody had ever heard of Francis
Kilvert, except members of his family and a few aged country-
folk or their descendants. Today it seems hardly necessary to
explain who he was, because he has come to be recognized as
one of the best of English diarists.

Kilvert's presentation of country days and ways in mid-
Victorian times is just as lifelike as what we find in novels of
the period, but as it is factual, and apparently perfectly truthful,
and full of well-observed detail, it gives, in a different way to that
of the novelists, an invaluable picture of day-to-day existence.
His Diary gives more than a picture, it creates an atmosphere,
and evokes what would now be called a life-style.

The Diary is much more than a source of social history.
Like the eminent novelists of his time, Kilvert was an artist.
He was a prose writer of distinction, and while writing enter-
tainingly about a variety of other people, he paints a self-
portrait of a fascinating man whom readers of the Diary get to
know with a special intimacy. A proof of his power to fascinate
those who read him is that the Kilvert Society, which has now
been flourishing for nearly a quarter of a century, has more than
six hundred members and keeps on growing.

Francis Kilvert, like Thomas Hardy, was born in 1840. He
was one of the six children of a country parson, the rector of
Hardenhuish, near Chippenham in Wiltshire. His father, the

Reverend Robert Kilvert, augmented his stipend, like a good
many other country clergymen in those days, by taking in
pupils. One of his pupils happened to be Augustus Hare, who
later became known as a writer of guide books and as a copious,
name-dropping, and gossipy writer of memoirs. It is now
fashionable to seek out instances of what is called the seamy
side of Victorian life, and Hare has left it on record that life
among the boys at Hardenhuish Rectory was not entirely
decorous:

> The first evening I was there, at nine years old, I was compelled
> to eat Eve's apple quite up—indeed, the Tree of knowledge of Good
> and Evil was stripped absolutely bare: there was no fruit left to
> gather.

The boys, according to Augustus Hare, were 'a set of little
monsters'. As for the rector, he was ultra-Evangelical, a dry
scholar, very hot-tempered, entirely without originality, and
with no knowledge either of the world or of little boys. He
punished his pupils ferociously and unjustly for exceedingly
slight offences; living under this reign of terror they learnt
nothing useful, and spent much time learning by heart the
Psalms and the Thirty-Nine Articles.

That was how Hare remembered life in the 1840s at Hardenhuish Rectory, but Kilvert later looked back upon it as what
he called his 'sweet old home', so perhaps the rector segregated
his sons from his pupils and gave them a less unpleasant time.
From there Kilvert went to a school near Bath kept by his
uncle, another parson, and then up to Oxford. He was ordained
when quite young, and spent a year acting as curate to his
father, who had moved to the neighbouring parish of Langley
Burrell.

At the age of twenty-four, he went as curate to the Reverend
Richard Lister Venables, the vicar of Clyro in Radnorshire.
Mr. Venables was more a man of the world than Kilvert's father,
and he had even travelled in Russia and had written a book
about it, which was published by the ever-distinguished firm
of John Murray. He was kind to Kilvert, so was his sympathetic
and understanding wife, and so were many people in the
neighbourhood, both of the landowning and the labouring
class. The surroundings of Clyro are beautiful, and Kilvert was
highly responsive to the landscape and to the Border people.
Not quite Welsh and not quite English, they have a delightful
character of their own, and round about Clyro they grew as

fond of Kilvert as he was of them. Altogether the seven years he spent there seem to have been the happiest of his life.

At the age of thirty-one, he went back as curate to his father in Wiltshire for another four years. He was then presented to a remote living in Radnorshire, and in the following year to that of Bredwardine, on the Wye in Herefordshire, not far from Clyro. Soon after this he married a young woman called Elizabeth Rowland: he was thirty-eight, she was twenty-two, and he had known her for three years. They went off to Scotland for their honeymoon and returned to an affectionate welcome from his parishioners at Bredwardine in a downpour of rain. This saturated the triumphal arches erected for the occasion, but did nothing to dampen the presents and speeches, and the warm-hearted villagers took the horses out of the carriage and themselves drew it to the vicarage.

Within a couple of weeks Kilvert was dead. He had died suddenly of peritonitis, no doubt the result of a ruptured appendix—those were the days before appendectomy. He was only thirty-eight, and the year was 1879. He was buried there at Bredwardine, and his young widow went home to Oxfordshire and her father, did good works in the parish, and lived on for more than thirty years. She had hoped to be buried beside him, but left her demise a little too long. Two maiden ladies had been inserted, one on each side of her late husband, so poor Mrs. Kilvert had to be deposited in a distant extension of the churchyard. It always seems to me that this circumstance might have furnished a motif for an ironical poem by Hardy.

Speaking of Hardy reminds me of a descriptive passage in Kilvert's Diary, which may well be called Hardyesque. In August 1873 Kilvert travelled up with Mr. and Mrs. Venables to a remote village in Radnorshire where a fete was being held.

While the athletic sports were going on, [he wrote] I wandered away by myself into congenial solitude for a visit to the ruined Church of Llanlionfel . . . The ruined Church tottered lone upon a hill in desolate silence. The old tombstones stood knee-deep in the long coarse grass, and white and purple flowers nodded over the graves. The door stood open and I went in. The window frames and seats were gone. Nothing was left but the high painted deal pulpit bearing the sacred monogram in yellow letters. Some old memorial tablets bearing Latin inscriptions in remembrance of Marmaduke Gwynne and his family were affixed to the East Wall. The place was utterly deserted, there was not a sound. But through the ruined windows I could see the white tents of the flower show in the valley beneath. I ascended the tall rickety pulpit and several white owls disturbed from their day sleep floated silently under the crazy Rood Loft on their broad downy wings and sauntered sailing without sound through the frameless east and west windows to take refuge with a graceful sweep of their broad white pinions in the ancient yew that kept watch over the Church. It was a place for owls to dwell in and for satyrs to dance in.

It is long since the Church has been used, though weddings were celebrated in it after it was disused for other services. There is a curious story of a gentleman who was married here. Some years after his marriage his wife died, and it happened that he brought his second bride to the same Church. Upon the altar rails she found hanging the lace handkerchief which her predecessor had dropped at the former wedding. The Church had never been used nor the handkerchief disturbed in the interval of years between the two weddings.

That evocation of a solitude shows how fitting it is that Kilvert's gravestone was inscribed with the words 'He being dead, yet speaketh': through his diary he not only speaks, but speaks with a living voice.

When the Diary came to light it was found to have been written in twenty-two notebooks, closely written in a conventional hand, with no margins, perhaps for economy's sake. It had apparently been kept continuously from January 1870 until five months before his wedding in 1879; but there were two large gaps, each of six months. The MS had been inherited by Kilvert's widow, and she is said to have destroyed the missing portions because she thought them too private and personal about herself. Not only about herself, perhaps. The first of them almost certainly contained some allusions to Kilvert's infatuation in Wiltshire with a handsome girl called Ettie Meredith-Brown. We know she was handsome because we have a photograph of her and also a description of her by Kilvert:

At 4 o'clock Miss Meredith-Brown and her beautiful sister Ettie came over to afternoon tea with us and a game of croquet. Ettie Meredith-Brown is one of the most striking-looking and handsomest girls whom I have seen for a long time. She was admirably dressed in light grey with a close fitting crimson body which set off her exquisite figure and suited to perfection her black hair and eyes and her dark Spanish brunette complexion with its rich glow of health which gave her cheeks the dusky bloom and flush of a ripe pomegranate. But the greatest triumph was her hat, broad and picturesque, carelessly twined with flowers and set jauntily on one side of her pretty dark head, while round her shapely slender throat she wore a rich gold chain necklace with broad gold links. And from beneath the shadow of the picturesque hat the beautiful dark face and the dark wild fine eyes looked with a true gipsy beauty.

We know that rather more than a year later Kilvert parted from this young woman with what he called a clinging embrace and passionate kiss, because there is an entry in the Diary which tells us so, an entry which perhaps escaped either his widow's eye or her scissors. We know from her photograph that Mrs. Kilvert, however amiable she may have been, was extremely unlike a ripe pomegranate, and it seems probable that she could not view with equanimity either her late husband's amorous confessions or the prospect of their being read by strangers. The second missing portion of the Diary presumably contained an account of Kilvert's courtship and his engagement to herself, and it is disappointing not to have it.

After the printed Diary had become famous, an old lady who had been brought up in what was already beginning to be called the Kilvert Country—that is, the border region of Herefordshire and Radnorshire—and who had been alive in his time, was asked, 'And what did your family think of Kilvert?' 'I don't suppose they thought of him at all', she rather snubbingly replied. 'After all, he was only the curate.' Only the curate! Now he is immortal, and they are forgotten.

There were legions of country curates in mid-Victorian days. We have it on the authority of Gladstone that, during the time when Kilvert was growing up, quite half the undergraduates at Oxford and Cambridge were reading for Holy Orders. Naturally curates, like other human species, were of widely varying characters and interests. No doubt some of them kept diaries, and no doubt most these were of very slight significance, full of ephemeral trivialities: most diaries are like that. I cherish a typical entry from an ordinary diary, kept in the present century:

Another miserable wet day, even wetter than yesterday. It is earnestly hoped that it will be less wet tomorrow.

Kilvert never wrote like that. It does seem wonderfully lucky that at least this one diary of exceptional interest and quality was kept in the 1870s by one country curate, and was eventually made public in the form of printed selections from what Mrs. Kilvert did not put in the fire. It is equally lucky that she did not put it all in the fire. I was told by a member of the

Kilvert family that there was always an understanding among them that Mrs. Kilvert did not wish the Diary to be preserved. Thanks to the initiative of a more imaginative and intelligent person, a nephew of Kilvert's, now long dead, the process of editing it for print became possible.

Something must now be said about the editing of diaries, and of this diary in particular. Experience suggests that few diaries are worth printing, and very few indeed worth printing in full. If Kilvert's Diary, even after the amputations by his widow, had been printed as it stood it would have filled nine volumes, and such a bulky and expensive book by a man nobody had heard of could hardly have found a publisher, let alone enough public libraries or private readers to buy it: but Jonathan Cape launched the Diary, at a time when the Second World War was coming up. An editor's responsibility, in abridging a diary, is to concentrate what seems most characteristic of the diarist and his world and most likely, for one reason or another, to be of special or general lasting interest. There are always persons who suggest that some of the editor's omissions must have been of a scandalous or pornographic nature. This is not true of Kilvert's Diary: what was left out of it was mostly trivial, repetitive, or judged not to be of special value. What was printed can be now read not in nine but in three volumes, or still further abridged in one volume in paperback.

Can one speak of 'the diary' as one speaks of 'the novel' as a literary form? If so, it is a most difficult form. A diary is so personal that its effectiveness is specially dependent upon the private character, and particularly the honesty, of the writer. A poem, a play, or a novel can or must be imaginative, invented, fanciful, indirect, but a diary is direct. The diarist speaks in his own person, mostly about what has just happened, a few hours or even a few minutes before, and of its immediate effect upon himself and others. So does a reporter, but a diarist is quite different. A reporter is subservient, as a rule, to an editor; he is looking for news of what he supposes to be of instant public interest, which generally seems to mean something as horrible or depressing as possible: but a diarist is independent, and is recording, as truthfully as he can, private matters, or a private view of public matters, which he presumably supposes may be of future or even of continuing interest.

A diarist living in close touch with persons of great political, social, artistic, or scientific position, or distinction, or influence, may well feel that what they do or say in private may be worth recording; a careerist might want to keep in his diary a proud and self-justifying account of his arrival on each successive rung of the ladder to fame and fortune; but the motives of either of these cannot be much like the motives of an obscure country curate in mid-Victorian England. For whom would such a man as Kilvert be keeping a diary? Was it for the benefit of his descendants, if he should ever have any? (In fact, he left none.) Was it to re-read in his old age? (In fact, he died in his thirties.) Was it because he had something sensational to record or confess? He made no such claim. Kilvert could not, I think, be called introspective or introverted, but he did once ask himself, in his Diary, why he was keeping it. This is what he wrote:

Why do I keep this voluminous diary? I can hardly tell. Partly because life appears to me such a curious and wonderful thing that it almost seems a pity that even such a humble and uneventful life as mine should pass altogether away without some such record as this, and partly too because I think the record may amuse and interest some who come after me.

There is the point. Everyday life did not seem to him ordinary or humdrum; even what he called the humble and uneventful seemed to him 'curious and wonderful', therefore enjoyable. His responses to it were evidently more alert and sensitive than those of the people around him. He wanted to record it, to give it a lasting shape, to communicate it to others, to entertain them. This was the impulse of an artist.

One stormy afternoon in March, a hundred years ago, he was out in the hills near Clyro, when the dark clouds suddenly and dramatically began to roll away as he was looking across to the Black Mountains. He describes in some detail the dazzling revelation of white snow in a burst of sunlight in the clear blue sky:

I never saw anything to equal it, I think, even among the High Alps. The sudden contrast was tremendous, electrifying. I could have cried with the excitement of the overwhelming spectacle. I wanted someone to admire the sight with me. A man came whistling along the road riding upon a cart horse. I would have stopped him and drawn his attention to the mountains but I thought he would probably consider me mad. He did not seem to be in the least struck by or to be taking the smallest notice of the great sight.

There is a curious parallel to this in another diary, an earlier one than Kilvert's. In fact it was written by a woman who lived not a hundred but a thousand years ago. She was Japanese, and her name was Sei Shōnagon. With a Kilvert-like attention to detail, she gives a beautiful account of raindrops sparkling on chrysanthemums and spiders' webs in the early sunshine of an autumn morning. 'I was greatly moved and delighted,' she says. 'Later I described to people how beautiful it all was. What most impressed me was that they were not at all impressed.'

This ancient diary was translated by that famous poet and orientalist, Arthur Waley, and it was from him that there came one of the greatest compliments yet paid to Kilvert. When Waley was on his death-bed in 1966, and in great pain, the book he wished to have read to him was Kilvert's Diary. After his death a passage was found sidelined in pencil and against it he had faintly written 'Like Chinese poem.'

What sort of man was Kilvert? His sensibility did not make him an aesthete or dilettante. He shows no knowledge or taste at all in architecture, painting, or music: one might say that his Diary is about people in a landscape; and surely that is mainly what makes a good diary—human interest in a particular environment, and a zest for life in the diarist. Kilvert's social status was that of a gentleman in Holy Orders, an educated man without private means. As a Churchman he had evidently been formed by his Evangelical father, but was ahead of his father in his ecumenical tendencies: he was capable of slipping into a Roman Catholic church to pray for Christians to be united. In those days a country parish was still a close community, and as a parish priest Kilvert was dutiful, devoted, and much loved.

His social and political views seem to have been conventional and unquestioning. He knew when local people had no blankets or boots or not enough to eat, and minded, and tried to help them, but except from hearsay he knew little, it seems, of industrial and urban miseries. He was conventionally patriotic, expressed no doubts about imperial expansion, and did not question the accepted ideas of the propertied class in which he moved as easily as among their tenantry. His status, his opinions, and his religion evidently gave him a sense of security, or at least of continuity. If he had no money, at least he knew where his next meal was coming from. A countrywoman whose mother had known and revered Kilvert once told me that when he had a chicken for his dinner he used to set aside half of it to take to some poor person who would be glad of it. This rather suggests St. Martin bisecting his cloak for the beggar.

What did Kilvert look like? We have his photograph in profile. He is seated on a chair, wearing a clerical black frock-coat and floppy trousers, practical boots, a white bow-tie, and a thick dark beard which is virtually a mask. His thick, dark hair is shiny with pomatum. The camera may not lie, but it can anaesthetize a sitter, and the face is all but expressionless. The nose is short and straight, the eyes are averted from the camera, and appear small. We know there was something troublesome about his eyes, but not whether it was temporary or permanent. His sight was excellent, but at one point he believes that a girl is fond of him in spite of what he calls 'my poor, disfigured eyes'. What did he mean? Did he have just then, perhaps, a stye, or something like conjunctivitis? There is no sign of disfigurement in the photograph.

An old cousin of Kilvert's remembered him as 'very sleek and glossy and gentle, rather like a nice Newfoundland dog'; and he must have had an attractive voice. His father, after listening to him in church one morning, said, 'As you were preaching there came back upon my ear an echo of the tones of the sweetest human voice I ever heard, the voice of John Henry Newman. No voice but yours ever reminded me of him.' But Kilvert's dulcet voice and glossy sleekness did not make him a softy. He was a considerable athlete, not that he was interested in sport, but he was a vigorous walker in the Welsh hills and mountains. In fact he had great energy and vitality. For most people, whether in Victorian or any other times, life is largely an endurance test, but Kilvert wrote in his Diary, 'It is a positive luxury to be alive.'

It may have been; but the situation of a young and healthy man with natural appetites, hedged in by the taboos of a non-permissive society, and in no position to live, like some Victorians, a double life, even if he had wanted to, was not easy. When Kilvert, in his Clyro days, wanted to marry a gentle girl of his own class called Daisy Thomas, he was headed off by his intended father-in-law, not because of his character but because he was a penniless curate without apparent prospects. Having described the interview, which is as good as something in a novel, he admits that at the time he had only one sovereign in his possession, and he owed that.

Kilvert was extremely susceptible, and was always in love with somebody. A few years ago Richard Hoggart remarked that 'Kilvert had an enormous capacity for love in all sorts of aspects—for sensuality, for tenderness, for regard and affection

. . . a sort of love flowed from his finger-ends.' He was obviously attractive, in a magnetic sort of way, and knew it. 'It is a strange and terrible gift,' he wrote, 'this power of stealing hearts and exciting such love.' He did excite love and affection among all sorts of people, old and young, and notably in very young girls. Like his contemporary, Lewis Carroll, Kilvert doted on young girls. He idealized them, sentimentalized over them, and responded so warmly to their playfulness that, even by present-day standards, he seems indiscreet. If there had been anything sinister in his attentions to them he would hardly have written so candidly in his Diary about his feelings. He could certainly have said, as Lewis Carroll once did, 'I am extremely fond of children, except boys.'

From his bedroom window in Clyro he had a view of a wooded hillside with a white farmhouse at the top, and when he looked up at it he used to think of a dairymaid who lived there. What he writes about her is not at all like a Chinese poem. Half erotic, half religious, it is a sort of Pre-Raphaelite rhapsody:

The sun looks through her window which the great pear tree frames and lattices in green leaves and fruit, and the leaves move and flicker and throw a chequering shadow upon the white bedroom wall, and on the white curtains of the bed. And before the sun has touched the sleeping village in the shade below . . . he has stolen into her bedroom and crept along the wall from chair to chair till he has reached the bed, and has kissed the fair hand and arm that lies upon the coverlet and the white bosom that heaves half uncovered after the restlessness of the sultry night, and has kissed her mouth whose scarlet lips, just parting in a smile and pouting like rosebuds to be kissed, show the pearly gleam of the white teeth, and has kissed the sweet face and the blue veined silky lashed eyelids and the white brow and the soft bright tangled hair, till she has unclosed the sweetest eyes that ever opened to the dawn, and risen and un-fastened the casement and stood awhile breathing the fresh fragrant mountain air as it blows cool upon her flushed cheek and her half-veiled bosom, and lifts and ruffles her bright hair which still keeps the kiss of the sun. Then when she had dressed and prayed towards the east, she goes out to draw water from the holy spring, St. Mary's Well. After which she goes about her honest holy work, all day long, with a light heart and a pure conscience.

Such fanciful reveries are rare in the Diary, which mostly tells of things seen and heard, not imagined. Kilvert was always out and about. He was constantly asked out to dinners and picnics, croquet parties and archery parties at local country houses, and was evidently a welcome guest. Most of his time was taken up with 'villaging', as he called it, walking all round the parish to visit often remote dwellings, to comfort the old and the sick and the poor and the mad and the lonely. Their lives were often grim, and there are tales of suicides and murders. Memories went back a long way. He used to talk to a veteran of the Peninsular War, and help him to dig up his potatoes; people would tell him anecdotes of Charles II or Cromwell; and old Hannah Whitney in Clyro could remember the talk of persons born in the early eighteenth or even the late seventeenth century, and could repeat their tales of the fairies in which they believed.

In the early part of the last century, before the Oxford Movement and the Evangelical revival had got under way, the Anglican religion had sunk, in some country places, into an extraordinary state of neglect. Kilvert now and then heard reminiscences of this:

Crichton said that old Boughrood Church was a most miserable place. The choir sat upon the altar and played a drum.

Then in Dorset:

The Vicar of Fordington told us of the state of things in his parish when he first came to it nearly half a century ago. No man had ever been known to receive the Holy Communion except the parson, the clerk, and the sexton. There were 16 women communicants and most of them went away when he refused to pay them for coming . . . At one church there were two male communicants. When the cup was given to the first he touched his forelock and said, 'Here's your good health, Sir.' The other said, 'Here's the good health of our Lord Jesus Christ.'
One day there was a christening and no water in the font.
'Water, Sir!' said the clerk in astonishment. 'The last person never used no water. He spit into his hand.'

Kilvert was not pompous about his religion, and has some lively anecdotes about mishaps or eccentricities in church and about a most remarkable hermit whom he calls the Solitary. And there is a charming little story about a child:

The Bishop of Worcester, who is singularly spare and attenuated, was staying in a house. He observed a child looking at him very attentively for some time, and when the Bishop left the room the child asked, 'Is the Bishop a spirit?' 'No, the Bishop is a very good man, but he is not exactly a spirit yet. Why do you ask?' 'Because', said the child gravely, 'his legs are so very thin, I thought no one but a spirit could have such very thin legs.'

Kilvert was not always stuck in one place. He visits London, Oxford, the Isle of Wight, Cornwall, Bath, and Bristol, and we know he visited Switzerland and France. In good repute among the local clergy, he was so well thought of at a higher, episcopal level that he was offered the chaplaincy at Cannes, which seems an unusual preferment for an unworldly and inconspicuous country parson. His diary at Cannes, in what would then have been to him an unfamiliarly grand, worldly, and cosmopolitan society, would have been worth having, but his heart would not have been in it. Cannes was, so to speak, in the Augustus Hare country, and Kilvert had lost his heart to the country people round Clyro and Bredwardine. Perhaps that was why he declined the offer.

Kilvert had a lively interest in poets and poetry, and the Diary has some interesting allusions to Wordsworth, and a valuable account of a visit to William Barnes in Dorset. He also wrote poetry himself, but his poems are quite without the sharp focus of his prose; they are soft-centred, and in form and diction show the typical weaknesses of the conventional minor verse of his time.

A man so fond of people and of chronicling their sayings and doings is unlikely to be perfectly solemn, and there is a good vein of humour in the Diary. There used to be a most delightful railway along the Wye Valley between Hereford and Brecon, and here is a delightful account of an old lady, Mrs. Dew, making an outing by train from Whitney-on-Wye to Hereford and proving rather a trial to her son, a clergyman:

At Whitney station Henry Dew and his mother, old Mrs. Dew, got into the train to go to Hereford. They wanted to go second class but one carriage was full of farmers and another was full of smoke generated by the two captains, so they went first class and paid the difference. While Mrs. Dew was standing upright in the carriage, the train snatched on suddenly, throwing her back breathless into her seat. The station master threw in a parcel of blankets after them and away they went, leaving on the platform a brace of rabbits which they were to have taken to the Frederick Dews. The rabbits were sent after them by the next train, but being insufficiently addressed and unable to find Mrs. Dew they came back by the train following.

Meanwhile Mrs. Dew in Hereford had been much discomposed and aggrieved because her sons Henry and Frederick would not allow her to spend more than an hour and a half at Gethin's the upholsterer's, a time in which Henry Dew said he could have bought the whole town. He declared he never was so glad to get away from anywhere as from Gethin's shop where young Gethin and four shopmen were all serving Mrs. Dew on the broad grin. Then Mrs. Dew bought a large bag of buns and sweets for her grand-children at Ayston Hill, the young Frederick Dews, but in the excitement of parting she forgot to leave the bag and brought it to Whitney. Then to crown all she was nearly driven over and killed by an omnibus in Broad Street. The omnibus came suddenly round a corner and she holloed at the driver and the driver holloed at her, the end of it being that she was nearly knocked down by the pole. Her son Henry saved her and told her she was not fit to go about Hereford by herself. She said she was. He said she thought she was ten years old and could go anywhere and was as obstinate as could be. While they were arguing a cab came round the corner and nearly knocked the old lady down again, 'There,' said her son, 'there you go again. Are you satisfied now?'

That might almost be a sequence from some farcical film. Mrs. Dew, by the way, had the unusual distinction of having been kissed by Coleridge when she was a baby, of having had a sonnet addressed to her by Wordsworth, and of having broken off an engagement to one of Wordsworth's sons.

In various parts of the Diary there are scenes, incidents, anecdotes, and characters which would have done very well in some novel by Trollope or Dickens or Hardy, and there is a remarkable set-piece about the death at Worcester of a relation of the Kilverts, about her will, and about what Kilvert and his parents found when they went to her house near the Cathedral to attend her funeral, and to find out how she had disposed of her property, and whether they had benefited, and to what extent, by the will. This is a wonderfully vivid scene from mid-Victorian life, told with that skill which proves Kilvert a prose writer of real accomplishment, with a sense of drama, of character, and of irony. If there is one thing about his prose which is conspicuous it is that not a word is wasted, there is no padding, all is clear and orderly. His father may have been a dry old scholar, but Francis Kilvert was no doubt given by his father a proper grounding in Latin; he was taught how to put a sentence or a sequence of sentences together; and his own feeling for words, his delight in finding the right words to shape and colour what he wanted to say, and his delight in life, save him from ever being dry or dull.

Throughout the Diary there are exact and beautiful pieces of description—not 'fine writing', but perfect writing. It was said by the late Humphry House that Kilvert's 'great virtue is the power of conveying the physical quality of everything he describes', and at times one is reminded that he lived in the same era as the French Impressionists. Here is his 'great virtue' in a single sentence:

The lurid copper smoke hung in a dense cloud over Swansea, and the great fleet of oyster boats under the cliff was heaving in the greenest sea I ever saw.

Kilvert had the good fortune to live in parts of the English or Welsh countryside which had, and still have, special beauties, and to be unusually aware of them. His England had its wrongs and its troubles, but the countryside did have a deep and ancient quietness which has gone for ever. Living before that horrible invention, the internal combustion engine, before the telephone, the radio, the aeroplane, and the pop festival, he experiences and continually fixes in words that marvellous lost peacefulness. If he had known that he was enjoying the great privilege of living in the last few remaining years of tranquillity he could not have taken more care to describe it.

Sometimes, on a quiet day in summer or autumn, the sort of day when any commonplace diarist would have felt that nothing whatever had occurred to write about, Kilvert would give a detailed account of what was to be seen or heard. Here is an example. April, 1870. It is Easter Eve in Clyro churchyard, and people are decorating the graves with primroses and other spring flowers:

More and more people kept coming into the churchyard as they finished their day's work. The sun went down in glory behind the dingle, but still the work of love went on through the twilight and into the dusk until the moon rose full and splendid. The figures continued to move about among the graves and to bend over the green mounds in the calm clear moonlight and warm air of the balmy evening.

At 8 o'clock there was a gathering of the choir in the church to practise the two anthems for tomorrow. The moonlight came streaming in broadly through the chancel windows. When the choir had gone and the lights were out and the church quiet again, as I walked down the churchyard alone the decked graves had a strange effect in the moonlight and looked as if the people had lain down to sleep for the night out of doors, ready dressed to rise early on Easter morning. I lingered in the verandah before going to bed. The air was as soft and warm as a summer night, and the broad moonlight made the quiet village almost as light as day. Everyone seemed to have gone to rest and there was not a sound except the clink and trickle of the brook.

Five years later, on an afternoon in May, Kilvert is at home in Wiltshire:

As I came down from the hill into the valley across the golden meadows and along the flower-scented hedges a great wave of emotion and happiness stirred and rose up in me. I know not why I was so happy, nor what I was expecting, but I was in a delirium of joy, it was one of the supreme few moments of existence, a deep delicious draft from the strong sweet cup of life.

By a complex of lucky chances, one man, evolved by a particular civilization, in a particular place and time, a man who had a healthy appetite for life and who was uncommonly articulate, left on record how the strong sweet cup of life tasted to him. By another tangle of lucky chances, we can escape into his lost world, now almost as remote as the world of a Chinese poem, though still just within living memory, and we can enter into it so closely that is seems to become part of our own experience.

THE WEDMORE MEMORIAL LECTURE

This lecture perpetuates the memory of Sir Frederick Wedmore, author and critic. It was founded by his daughter, Miss Millicent Wedmore, a member of this Society from 1928 until 1964

THE FILM OF THE BOOK

By DILYS POWELL, C.B.E., F.R.S.L.

(Read 12 April 1973)

Robert Speaight, C.B.E., F.R.S.L., in the Chair

ONE of the first films I ever saw was *The Last Days of Pompeii*. I was taken to see it in my childhood; I fancy it was an Italian version, and certainly it was silent. I was disagreeably impressed. Possibly the excitement was too much for me; anyway I remember begging my parents not, in future, to take me to the cinema. However, I must have recovered, for presently I went with my mother to see a film of Marie Corelli's *The Sorrows of Satan*. My family on the distaff side were much addicted to Marie Corelli. Searching through the handbooks, I find that the great D. W. Griffith made a version of *The Sorrows of Satan*, but the one I saw was earlier; I feel sure of that. By the time of the Griffith version I had already sat through *The Birth of a Nation* and *Intolerance*—sat bewildered, for my family were long-sighted and chose to occupy seats at the back of the hall, a position from which I could scarcely distinguish the outlines of the screen. Later, having I suppose insisted on a closer approach, I wept and suffered through *Orphans of the Storm* and *Broken Blossoms*. By 1926, the date of Griffith's Corelli film, I was beginning to know the names of the players and, occasionally, of the directors; by then the version of *The Sorrows of Satan* which I saw (at the time I thought it a work of high integrity and deep compassion) must have vanished into the shadowy world haunted by so many earnest, touchingly naïve works of the early and the middle period of silence.

I must not exhaust you with the catalogue of the other films which marked my apprenticeship to the screen—*Lorna Doone*,

Ben-Hur, The Dumb Girl of Portici, Cabiria (d'Annunzio was co-author of the script of *Cabiria*), *Quo Vadis*—no, not *Quo Vadis*; the primitive versions of that belong to the period when I asked my parents to let me stay at home. I may have been influenced by more than a shrinking from blood and circuses. In days when I would work through the small advertisements in a newspaper rather than read nothing, a copy of the works of Sienkiewicz must have fallen into my hands, for I distinctly recall a story in which a leading character got his come-uppance in a giant pestle and mortar, and possibly that contributed to my stay-at-home mood. Anyway it was not until decades later that I was at last subjected to the gladiatorial horrors, the crucifixions and Christian-eating lions of *Quo Vadis*, and I mention the title in this context only as an indication of an embryonic relationship between literature—well, at any rate written fiction—and the screen.

The silent cinema, of course, produced many creators who did not rely for their material on the written word. The great comics—in America Chaplin, Keaton, Harold Lloyd; in France Max Linder—usually invented their own jokes or collaborated with professional script-writers and gag-men; you will scarcely ever find any connection between their famous films and the books or plays of their time or any other time. The directors of serious films, on the other hand—serious, that is, in mood, for comedy, after all, is a very serious business—were not always as self-reliant. D. W. Griffith based *Broken Blossoms* on a story by Thomas Burke, *The Birth of a Nation* itself was drawn from a novel by Thomas Dixon called *The Clansman*—though one does rather wonder whether the novelist would have recognized his own work.

Perhaps from the authors of some of the titles I have mentioned—Bulwer Lytton, Marie Corelli, General Lew Wallace (who wrote *Ben-Hur*)—you will be inclined to draw certain conclusions about what books were being read at the time such films were being made; and it is true that throughout the history of the cinema there has been an interesting relationship between public taste in literature and public taste in films. I should point out that the family expeditions to the cinema of which I have spoken were made in what was then a quiet, provincial seaside town where the theatre afforded little more than a pantomime at Christmas and an occasional touring company—the Benson group in Shakespeare, Martin Harvey in *The Only Way*. We lived happily—a bit bored, I dare say, but still happily—in an aesthetic backwater. I doubt, though, whether the level of our entertainment would have been very different if we had been frequenting a metropolitan cinema and not our local Electric Theatre, as it was called. We were still in the age of reading not so much the classics (though Scott and, thank heavens, Dickens were always with us) as the decent solid nineteenth-century novel or the decent boys' adventure book: the age of peaceful Sundays and taking a book for the afternoon out of a cupboard normally kept locked.

It was an age, too, when every middle-class provincial family knew something about the Bible and had a vague idea that the Romans, what with Pontius Pilate, not to mention all those mysterious orgies, really deserved everything they got at Pompeii. (The Greeks? Nobody ever mentioned them.) As for religion, it may have been a matter of moral obligation, of Sunday observance and not much more, but at least it was a kind of pavement to our modest lives. The cinema very rightly recognized that, and returned again and again to the themes of both the Old and the New Testament. Much later in the history of the screen the gigantic figures of Biblical myth—or rather Biblical history, for archaeology has taught us that myth is merely history with gold trimmings—were exploited in films of adventure, spectacle and sensationalism. In the early days the screen did no more than supply a response to the desire of the public to see the Bible tales sentimentally re-created. Only D. W. Griffith, recognizing the tragedy in the story of the fall of Babylon, with *Intolerance* added something like majesty to the myth.

Perhaps I am giving the impression of a cinema catering for an evangelical society, a society which required entertainment on a high moral but a low literary level. I must be careful. It is true that the screen, having climbed out of its fairground origins (for one must remember that it began as a peepshow, an extension of What the Butler Saw), did indeed in its first stages aim at an audience little acquainted with the works of Oscar Wilde or, come to that, of Joseph Conrad (*An Outcast of the Islands*, though it was not to be filmed until more than half a century later, appeared at almost the same time as the first manifestation of cinematography). The cinema in its angel-infancy was more nearly akin to an audience which had read *The Lamplighter*, *Christie's Old Organ*, and *Jessica's First Prayer*, works of the imagination probably not familiar to members of The Royal Society of Literature. Nevertheless the screen from time to time had visions of higher things, especially in Italy. In 1908 an Italian director was already making a version of *Hamlet*. There was a *Romeo and Juliet* in the same year; a year later a *Macbeth*; and in 1910 another *Hamlet*. It is doubtful whether any of these Shakespearean essays ran for much more than ten minutes. In 1915, however, one of the legendary British Shakespearean actors, Forbes-Robertson, appeared in a three-reel film of *Hamlet*; even so the tragedy must have been over and done with, ghost, duels and all in about half an hour.

No matter; it was, it always is the thought which counts. But somehow at that moment in history the thought failed to count. It failed to count aesthetically and intellectually. In spite of all the Shakespeare—and I must add in spite of the imaginative endeavour, in spite of the infant genius, a new kind of genius, which was invigorating the screen—the cinema was still looked on as low-class. When the President of the United States (it was Woodrow Wilson) saw *The Birth of a Nation* he said it was 'like writing history in lightning'. And so it was; and perhaps in the United States public opinion was sufficiently advanced and sufficiently flexible to recognize that a major form of narrative was on its way. After all it was in the United States that a poet, Vachel Lindsay, early on saw the cinema as an important recruit to the world of the arts. I am bound to admit that, looking back, I find this country guilty of appalling snobbery about the screen.

I suppose that if you take a film as simply a translation of a book or a play—and that is how a great many people used to look at it and probably still look at it—the cinema can dwindle to the fourth-rate. I believe that the screen, though it may not succeed in doing everything that a novel can do, is capable of creative achievements which are entirely its own. Of course if you look at a silent film of, say, *Bleak House*, or *Anna Karenina*, or even something as comparatively uncomplicated as *Dr. Jekyll and Mr. Hyde*, you are likely to compare it unfavourably with the precisely used phrases, the literary subtleties of its original. The screen tried, however, to compensate. One must remember that the silent cinema was never really silent. It had music. For an important, big-scale production there would be an orchestra supplied with a score especially selected and arranged with cues. But even the simplest film would be accompanied by a pianist, sitting watchful at his instrument, sometimes improvising but always suiting the tune to the action; he had at his disposal collections of music applicable to a variety of moods and divided into sections under such headings as 'mysterioso' or 'agitato'; or of course there was 'hurry music'.

In another sense as well the silent cinema was never silent. It used words, and not only the words which exhorted ladies to remove their hats. As, illustrating the dialogue with gestures and facial expressions, the players mouthed or appeared to be mouthing significant phrases, the lines would appear in print, usually in précis form. A famous example is often quoted: Theda Bara, most celebrated of the vamps, is addressing her victim in a piece called *A Fool There Was*. 'Kiss me,' she says, 'my Fool!' Again, the screen would offer a kind of stage direction, an indication of a situation or a mood. 'Came the dawn', it would announce when the heroine, as heroines in those days so often did, had stooped to folly. Sometimes these titles, as they were called, were illustrated. Alfred Hitchcock began his career in films by supplying the necessary drawings. 'For instance,' he says—I quote from the long dialogue recorded by the French director François Truffaut—'For instance, if the line read: "George was leading a very fast life by this time", I would draw a candle, with a flame at each end, just below the sentence. Very naïve' he adds. Only too often, in fact, the words instead of elevating the cinema served to emphasize, I will not say its illiteracy but what to many spectators must have seemed its elementary nature.

You may think that I am speaking merely of the primitive fictions of the screen. But the use of descriptive and other titles persisted; you will find them in the mature silent films of Chaplin or of Harold Lloyd. 'Step right up', Lloyd invites his unwelcoming contemporaries in a college film, or rather we read that he is inviting them, 'Step right up and call me Speedy!' Titles were still there in the best of Buster Keaton, in *The General*, and you can't go higher than that. At the very end of the silent period the German cinema began trying to do without them: in, for instance, *The Last Laugh*. Whether the screen could have gone much farther without titles is doubtful. Nevertheless the intellectual devotees—for by the end of the nineteen-twenties the intellectual audience had got round to the screen—were claiming that the cinema was a purely visual medium. But, as I say, it used words. And if I have dwelt on what must seem a tenuous connection with dialogue and verbal description it is because I feel that the narrative cinema always from its beginnings, except in experimental essays, maintained some kind of relationship with the written word.

All the same when the first talkies appeared there was an outcry. Purity had been violated.

It is perfectly true that at first cinematography seemed to have forgotten everything it had learned. In an effort to master the new technique of sound, films drifted into the manner of photographed plays, and bad plays at that. Perhaps the new snobbery was understandable—not the snobbery which looked down on the cinema as an entertainment for the illiterate, but a snobbery which refused to admit technical expansion. Many critics and historians were convinced that speech had ruined everything. They refused to admit that the main stream of the cinema had never been pure, that it had always been a hybrid needing words, and that by embracing dialogue it was very properly extending its capacities as a narrative, an instructive, a descriptive or an exploratory form. And however much before the admission of the talkies the screen had owned to a faint connection with the novel or the play it was not, I think, until the end of the nineteen-twenties and the beginning of the nineteen-thirties that the relationship of book and film could be seriously examined. Before then words were employed under sufferance. Since then they have been in partnership.

For a little less than half a century, then, it has been possible to make a valid comparison of a film and a book—or a play, for in this context I hope one may include the drama as well as the novel and the short story. In fact one must, one really must include Shakespeare; for in its treatment of Shakespeare the cinema has encountered its most distinguished, its most high-class criticism. We can forget those early, speechless, ten-minute scampers through the plots of *Hamlet*, or *King Lear*, or *Julius Caesar*. I leave aside, also, though it is an early talkie, the 1929 film of *The Taming of the Shrew* with Mary Pickford, Douglas Fairbanks—and a credit title which has given much pleasure over the years: 'By William Shakespeare,' it said, 'with additional dialogue by Sam Taylor.' I am not myself affronted by the idea of that additional dialogue. One does not need to be a campaigner for Women's Lib. to decide that one can live without *The Taming of the Shrew*. There have even been times when I thought the Cole Porter musical *Kiss Me Kate* was an improvement on the original. In any case I do not propose to join in the sport of baiting the less literate movies; more worthwhile to try to see where in their direct relationship with literature they have failed, where succeeded—and where success or failure has resulted from something inherent in the nature of the medium itself.

It is easy to forget how many Shakespeare films there have been since the screen began to speak. I can think of three *Othellos*, for instance, one of them from Russia, and four versions of *Macbeth*, one of them from Japan. I recall three films of *Romeo and Juliet*—and I am not counting the parasitic pieces such as the musical *West Side Story* or a bizarre essay in gangster cinema called *Joe Macbeth*. I suppose the first of the straightforward adaptations of a Shakespeare play to persuade one that it really was Shakespeare, that one was hearing the Shakespearean poetry and watching the Shakespearean characters, was *Henry V*, just at the end of the Second War.

I am discounting an *As You Like It* which, though it gave us the young Laurence Olivier as Orlando, gave us also a Rosalind with an accent far from English; and I am discounting the *Romeo and Juliet* made in 1936 in the United States because in spite of a certain Hollywood opulence and elegance its chief performers, even the graceful Leslie Howard, never took fire. To *Henry V* one went with misgivings—but stayed with rising excitement. For here one recognized that the potentialities of the cinema could be used to do more than give an honest but flat translation; they could contribute to understanding and appreciation. I am not thinking simply of the cavalry charge at Agincourt with its splendid handling of rhythm and accelerating pace (and with the Walton music). I am not thinking even of the use of colour, the sad muted colours of the English camp on the eve of battle and the brilliant defiant colours of the battle array itself. The stage might parallel that dramatic contrast. Where the film does, I think, make one look again, perhaps a little startled, is in the transition from an artificial setting to the limitless freedom of the screen. At the beginning the players are on stage at the Globe Theatre in the year 1600; but by subtle degrees we—and they—are transported *via* stylized architecture and a stylized landscape to the realism of a scene which makes that cavalry charge possible. And where the film impels one to listen again, perhaps to think again, is in the handling of soliloquy. 'Upon the king!'—the young Henry's voice speaks, but not the lips; we overhear, as it were, the thoughts. The cinema uses its own artifice to interpret the artifice of Elizabethan drama.

You may say that *Henry V* is a comparatively simple play full of incident, dependent on action, and therefore readily shaped for the purposes of the screen; and so it is—at any rate so it seems now that we have seen it done. Perhaps one ought to consider a film of a more difficult play, a more complex example of the Shakespearean drama; and that is exactly what the people who made *Henry V* proceeded to do. They considered a work which has been endlessly argued over, which has been interpreted in a dozen different ways, and which is so long that on the stage it is scarcely ever seen complete. They considered *Hamlet*. And the result is especially interesting because it demonstrates both the capabilities of the screen and the difficulties encountered in dealing with a classic on a vast scale.

Possibly to those less enamoured of the cinema than I am the difficulties offer the more seductive theme. I am sure you do not need to be reminded that the producer, the director and the hero of the *Hamlet* film, as of *Henry V*, was Laurence Olivier, and that in both cases the text was edited by Alan Dent; some also of the same artists in setting and design (and the same musical composer) were involved. The film, in short, was made by people who were steeped in Shakespeare and had, as it were, lived with the play. Probably that made them more conscious of the problems, more reluctant, shall I say, to introduce 'additional dialogue'. In *Henry V*, as a matter of fact, there had been a snatch of additional dialogue. Alan Dent, who added it, says none of the critics noted that he had given Pistol a couple of lines by Marlowe.

> Is it not passing brave to be a King
> And ride in triumph through Persepolis?

The lines come, as I am sure you will immediately recognize, from *Tamburlaine*; and no, I did not notice the interpolation. All that happened was that in some perverse way when I saw *Tamburlaine* played at the Old Vic those were the lines which struck most keenly on my ears.

With *Hamlet* it was a matter not of adding but of removing lines (there were considerable excisions in *Henry V* too). An English cinema audience, it seems, could not be trusted, any more than an English theatre audience, to sit quietly through the four hours or so needed for the tragedy complete. Erich von Stroheim once took a novel by Frank Norris, *McTeague*, and turned it into a film, *Greed*, nine hours long. It was too much for the faint-hearted audience—or rather for the distributors. The piece was reduced to two hours, and the complete version survived only in fragments—script, stills, rescued by scholars of the screen. Only the Russians are stout enough to watch a film of, for example, *War and Peace* which lasts pretty well an entire day. The adapters of *Hamlet* got the play down to two hours and thirty-five minutes (the Russians later made a version, a very fine one, which ran just five minutes less). Abbreviation meant ruthless cutting. Not only lines were left out, but scenes; not only scenes, but characters. You will not find Rosencrantz and Guildenstern in the film. Fortinbras has vanished, and with him Hamlet's soliloquy 'How all occasions do inform against me' after the passage of the army from Norway. For once even the most ill-read of us can recognize the excisions and the alterations, for Alan Dent, explaining and defending them in an introduction to his published text, has given us the entire play with the omitted passages enclosed in brackets. Time, as he points out, is the great abbreviator.

Today, in the nineteen-seventies, audiences have grown accustomed to enormously long films. They were less tolerant in 1948 when Olivier's *Hamlet* appeared. They were also less well prepared for the difficult and the obscure. Taste has moved in two directions. On the one hand it demands more violence. On the other it is quicker to seize a reference or to follow an experiment, better equipped to apprehend some elusive narrative argument. An intellectual approach has been required of a public which once, except for a few enthusiasts, felt called on to make only an emotional response. A good many of the emendations to Shakespeare which a quarter of a century ago teased the minds and consciences of Laurence Olivier and his textual editor would seem needless today. 'Meagre rites' for 'maimed rites', 'allow' for 'beteem'—

> . . . so loving to my mother
> That he might not beteem the winds of heaven
> Visit her face too roughly.

Nobody now would boggle over the original phrases; in fact I think 'beteem' was the word used by Nicol Williamson, playing the Prince, in Tony Richardson's film of the Round House production of *Hamlet*. With the Olivier *Hamlet* it was splendid acting, it was devotion to the play, it was the spirit of Shakespeare himself which made the film accessible to a large general public, not the concessions offered to the inexperienced. The textual adaptation was sensitive and skilful and scholarly. But when one looks back one sees that what gave the piece the air sometimes of a triumph and sometimes of a failure proceeded from the nature of cinema itself and from the way that nature was used or misused. There are passages where this

Hamlet insists unecessarily on the visual tradition of the
medium, passages where the audience is shown events which
the unassisted verse makes heartbreakingly clear. As if it were
not enough to listen to the Queen's speech about the death of
Ophelia, we have also to be shown the stream, the flowers, the
floating, drowning girl. And this, I think, is to misuse the
peculiar gifts of the cinema.

On the other hand the screen can make its own contribution
to Shakespeare. Sadly, long tracts have been excised from
Hamlet's talk with the visiting Players. But a moment of
extraordinary imagination has been added. The Ophelia of the
film is a fair-haired Ophelia. In his instruction to the Players
Hamlet takes in his hands the dark head of the boy who is the
Player Queen and pulls over it a flaxen wig; and whatever the
screen may actually show one knows, as the boy looks up,
that the Prince of Denmark sees the face of the Ophelia who
he believes has betrayed him.

I have selected these two Shakespearean films because they
were the first to convince me that Shakespeare was not an
impossible territory for the cinema; and *Hamlet* in particular
has occupied me because it offers what amounts to an illustrated
handbook on the relations between literature and the screen.
Since then there has been a great variety of Shakespearean
films. Olivier thought of tackling *Macbeth*. That was left to
others; but instead he gave us a brilliant *Richard III* which used
to astonishing effect the intimacy of cinematography. The
audience was not separated from the action, the audience was
involved in the action. It is one of the special talents of the
screen that it can draw the spectator into a scene and let him
move about in it; Olivier took his audience into his company
a swell as his confidence. I think it was this feeling of the con-
fidential which distinguished *Richard III* from the Shakespearean
films which were to follow, though there were some good ones.
From America came a *Julius Caesar* with a magnificent Cassius
from John Gielgud—and with the emphasis on the characters,
not, as people are inclined to expect in the cinema, on the action.
The Russian version of *Hamlet* took advantage of the power of
the screen to add depth to background. This was a Court which
had business beyond the obsessions of its Prince; you were not
merely looking in from the outside, you had the sensation of
spying from within and overhearing its official conversations.

Beside the analytical films of Shakespeare there are the
straightforward reproductions of stage performances. Olivier's

superb *Othello*, for instance, was translated from the National Theatre to the screen—not entirely as a photographed play but without much pretence at a cinematic style. I have to admit that the successful Shakespearean films have usually owed much of their success to players and directors with long stage experience. One can recall a handful of versions made with famous film stars and indeed with reverence for their source. But reverence is not enough; and more often than not those are the films, educational no doubt, which come out dead from the text up.

And now I think of a film not marked by notable reverence for the text; at any rate it got through *Othello* in an hour and a half. It was made in Paris and Rome, Viterbo and Perugia, Morocco and Venice. Money would run out. One of the several actresses cast to play Desdemona would take another job. The costumes would fail to turn up—and so would the director—Michael MacLiammoir tells the story in his entrancing book *Put Money in Thy Purse*. Time passed; rumours flew; one began to doubt whether one would ever see the film. But this was Orson Welles's *Othello;* and when at last, years later, it appeared in London one felt, truncated text or no, that one was seeing the essence of Shakespeare. It is years since I watched the film, but I remember the Moor walking with Iago through a long net of shadows; one knew, one saw that he was trapped. I remember half a dozen cruel and erotic and beautiful images; I remember an Italian, a Renaissance Othello. Welles and his team of artists were not attempting an illustration of the tragedy, poetry accompanied by appropriate pictures. They were attempting a partnership between words and images. There is no denying that in the chaotic conditions in which the film was shot the words sometimes came off second-best and poetry was sometimes sacrificed. Nevertheless an imagination which was both pictorial and literary had caught something of the genius of Shakespeare. I know that I have not found many people to agree with me about Welles's *Othello*, and I can understand the exasperation of those who feel that the text should always be sacred. At the same time I think one has to be wary of what I will call the looking-glass approach to the cinema. Perhaps today fewer people than formerly come away from a film complaining that it was not identical with the book on which it was based. That attitude belongs to a period when the cinema was still a poor relation of the arts, when it had not yet won the right to make its own rules. Certainly there have been times when the complainants had justice on their side. Lured, perhaps, by the resemblance of a film title to the title of an autobiographical book by Yeats-Brown, they might have been disconcerted to find themselves watching Gary Cooper having lighted tooth-picks stuck under his finger-nails. Nowadays when the cinema has become the province of young intellectuals such misapprehensions are less likely.

Nevertheless the literary fallacy persists. It can affect the judgment of any of us. Not long ago I for one was enraged by a version of *Women in Love* because I thought the interpretation of the character of Hermione horribly false to the D. H. Lawrence figure—and worse than false to the memory of Ottoline Morrell, on whom the figure was based. It is difficult to rid oneself of prejudice where a favourite author is concerned. With a writer by whose work one is not completely bewitched it is easy. One can remain calm over the adaptation of a novel by Harold Robbins: *The Carpetbaggers*, perhaps. Even disrespect to a classic can be endured. Personally I could tolerate ill-treatment of *Quentin Durward*. I confess to a vague dislike of an American film of *Ivanhoe* (though by now I recall little beyond a parade of horses in skirts and a good deal of bashing about with spiked ball-and-chain); but I was able to contain the desire to rush home and refresh myself at source.

Naturally it is all a matter of personal literary taste. Some years ago a stir was caused in France by a film of a famous eighteenth-century novel, Choderlos de Laclos's *Les Liaisons Dangereuses*. The record of elegantly vicious seduction had been brought up to date; the seducer followed his prey to the ski-ing slopes, messages of love were transmitted by tape-recorder, virtue deflowered learned the worst by telegram. The cinema is a great educator, and it drove me to read the book, of which I had up to then been totally ignorant. I thought the film—it was directed by Roger Vadim, creator of the Brigitte Bardot myth— an austere and fastidiously proportioned essay in style. But then I had not been brought up in horrified respect for the tarnished civilities of eighteenth-century French fiction. I had no pre-conceptions about the characters, their actions, or their social significance. It is when some adored masterpiece is concerned, some novel, perhaps, with which one has lived all one's life, that heat is engendered.

I have already remarked that there is a link between the reading habits of the general public and the films likely to be made. It is no longer fashionable to read Dickens, and with a

few exceptions Dickens novels are not at present often translated to the screen. One notes the exceptions: *A Christmas Carol*
is easy and turns up in various forms—including an animated
film made by Dick Williams and notable both for its fidelity and
for the warmth of its fancies. *Oliver Twist*, again, is comparatively
easy; its uncomplicated narrative, its elements of the grotesque
and the melodramatic lend themselves to the cinema. There has
even been a musical *Oliver Twist*, first on the stage and then on
the screen (it is one of the puzzles of cinematography that while
a plain adaptation of a classic may evoke bellows of rage, the
adaptation with song-and-dance can often do what it likes without attracting complaints). *Great Expectations*, too, has few of the
complexities of the grand, the massive Dickens novels. It has
also less of the emotional warmth; and David Lean was able, in
a memorable version made soon after the Second War, to pare
it down to a manageable narrative and characters reasonably
developed.

But much of the richness of Dickens is in occasional figures,
incidents, descriptions, ironic comments which, though they
all have their bearing on mood and movement, are as it were
offered free, generous gifts accompanying the basic creation.
The danger is not leaving too much out but putting too
much in, persevering, as one version of *Nicholas Nickleby*
persevered, with a scrapbook of Dickensian oddities, so that
the figures crowd against one another, overlay one another,
obliterate one another. The *Nicholas Nickleby* film gave us, of
course, Sir Mulberry Hawk; but for good measure Lord
Verisopht was there as well. Rightly the Squeers lot were
present in force, and the Mantalinis; but it was thought not
enough to show the Crummles family complete, we had to watch
the Infant Phenomenon being pursued by the Indian Savage.
In a film of the length normal at the time—*Nicholas Nickleby*
was made in the late nineteen-forties—there was no room for
such a host of eccentrics, at any rate no room to show them in
the round. They appeared, they vanished, and in the press of
incidents the narrative backbone was broken and the essential
feeling was lost.

Perhaps the best of Dickens is unattainable in a single film.
David Copperfield, I think, is among the more controllable.
I know that except for one or two portrait sketches—Olivier
and Attenborough, for example, as Creakle and Tungay—the
latest version was pretty dull. A much earlier attempt, though,
with W. C. Fields and Freddie Bartholomew, made a fair shot.

But *David Copperfield* has a strong spinal column. Thinking of the novel one thinks first of the central narrative and only second of the great grotesques clustering round it. I still fancy that the best of Dickens—and for me *David Copperfield* does not belong to the best—like *The Forsyte Saga* should be presented in short parts separated by the passage of time; much of Dickens, after all, first appeared piecemeal. Or perhaps an experiment might be made with the method adopted by the Russians for the translation of Tolstoy of which I have already spoken. *War and Peace* became an eight-hour film, but was divided into four parts which could be seen one at a time. Russian audiences, I believe, sometimes saw it at a sitting. The London critics, too, were given the full treatment—or nearly full. Entertained by an all-day sitting of a slightly contracted version, they emerged with the sensation, innocuous but vivid, of mild shell-shock. One recalls beautiful moments, but more war than peace: explosions, charges, wheeling armies, the appalling spectacle of battle. Tolstoy has size, and size was there; fidelity too; the Russians take few liberties with their classics. But to be honest one could have done with the taking of a liberty here and there. The more one sees of the cinema in its relations with literature the more one understands that it is not precise reproduction which counts but mood, the spirit of the original— that spirit which needed to be captured and so blithely escaped from *Nicholas Nickleby*.

And like reverence, fidelity cannot snare the spirit. Probably nobody has been completely successful with the grand-scale Russian works—with, for instance, Dostoevsky. It is not only the Russians who have tried. The French have made films of *The Idiot* and *Crime and Punishment*. Hollywood has tackled *The Brothers Karamazov*; I cannot claim that a fairly recent Russian version was a great deal better than the American one: impeccably played in a high theatrical style, shying away from some of the Alyosha episodes but otherwise clinging doggedly to its original, it rarely got off the solid Russian ground. And one is driven to the conclusion that fidelity can be worse than impiety. It can be too much; it can devitalize. And referring once again to Dostoevsky I think of two versions of his *White Nights*. The first, by Luchino Visconti, had an autumnal quality which deserved more than the grudging recognition it received; nevertheless there was something uncomfortably stagey about the film. The second was made by the French director Robert Bresson. Called *Four Nights of a Dreamer*, the story of the girl waiting for her lost lover was set in the Paris of today, with young people singing on the quays as the lights of the *bateaux-mouches* pass up and down the river. It was not a reproduction. It was a re-creation; remote, a hallucination, it gave a new enigmatic life to its theme.

It would be wrong, though, to conclude that the Russian cinema never brings imagination to the translation of the Russian classics. True that after the inventions which accompanied the first decade of the Revolution—and startled the world of cinematography—the creative impulse faltered. Under Stalin the revolutionary genius was stifled, to be replaced by nationalist propaganda, not to mention the cult of personality. In any case the major works of Eisenstein and Pudovkin and Dovzhenko had their roots in revolution rather than in literature. There are lyrical passages in *The Battleship Potemkin*, but the general effect is violent, shattering; I am tempted to use a word much favoured by the cinema in recommending some simple exercise in multiple murder, epic. Years were to go by before the Soviet screen was again allowed the freedom to celebrate private life instead of the national image; the habit of size, of making films about vast historical movement persisted.

But in the middle of a generalization I am pulled up short by a name: Maxim Gorky. One of Pudovkin's most famous films, *Mother*, was based on Gorky. And just before the Soviet Union was embroiled in the Second World War Gorky's autobiographical writings inspired another director, Mark Donskoi, to set to work on a trilogy: *My Childhood, My Apprenticeship, My Universities*. Watching, one felt one was seeing pre-revolutionary Russia, squalor and drunkenness and brutality irradiated by generosity and hope. The grandmother steadfast amidst the avarice and the callousness of a decaying household; the young Gorky arguing in the bakery cellar with his boss about the dignity of man while the workmen stir from their sleep on benches and tables to listen—it is the beginning of a wandering, self-educating life; and always insistently present is the enormous, pacific landscape, the river, the distances into which the sad, shackled convicts vanish. And again what is important is not the precision of incident, though I daresay that is present, but the mood, the feeling of a society soon to be driven by desperation towards change, towards a frightening upheaval. And the sense of human relationships—one cannot forget the touching passage in which an old man in hospital is overcome with pity for the young man who had so little pity for himself that he tried to commit suicide.

Maxim Gorky is among the writers who lend themselves readily to the cinema (both the French and the Japanese have made versions of *The Lower Depths*). So, unexpectedly perhaps, is Chekhov. He does not lend himself so readily outside Russia— nor always inside it either; there has been at any rate one dull Russian film of a Chekhov play. But I am thinking rather of the short stories, in particular of *The Lady with the Little Dog*. What happens in the story? A middle-aged married man, Gurov, on holiday at Yalta, is attracted by a young married woman, Anna; he is experienced, he seduces her, he thinks nothing of the affair —then he painfully discovers that both of them love one another irredeemably and that there is no way out. You could say that nothing happens, nothing in the sense by which a film is custo- marily judged: no violent action, no smart finale. And yet, every- thing happens, everything which makes up the business of living.

The film is remarkably faithful to its original; it never shrinks from the prosaic, undramatic, unaesthetic detail. Chekhov describes the woman sitting, after the seduction, with her long hair hanging down on both sides of a face 'drooped and faded'. There is a water-melon on the table. Gurov, Chekhov says, 'cut himself a slice and began eating it without haste'. It is all there on the screen, the dishevelled hair, the face fallen from its innocent freshness, the man's casual gesture with the melon. Fidelity, yes, but a great deal more is implied—remorse and shame for the woman, indifference for the man, the melancholy pause consequent on an irrevocable action. And now and then the film suggests some tiny detail in itself creative. In the foyer of the provincial theatre where Gurov has been against his judgement drawn to look for Anna a ridiculously posing figure sharpens the mournful irony of the situation. Again, the lovers, meeting secretly in a Moscow hotel, realize the dilemma of their lives; 'the most complicated and difficult part of it', says the concluding sentence of the story, 'was only just beginning'. In the last shots of the film they look out of the window to see an old street musician who plays a sad tune. He picks up from the snow the coins they throw to him; and in his humility, in the view of their figures at the high barred window, there is a kind of heartbreak.

Looking at *The Lady With the Little Dog*—and for me it is one of the best films ever made—I feel that it might have been written for the cinema.

I have the same feeling about some of the stories of Maupassant—not so much *Boule de Suif*, though the Russians made a good, small film of that, much better than one produced by the French. I am thinking rather of *A Country Excursion*, which Jean Renoir translated into the beautiful *Partie de Campagne*. I saw the film before I had read the story, and now I think of *Partie de Campagne* not in terms of Maupassant's supremely economical prose but in the images of the screen. Jean Renoir is the son of Auguste Renoir, and in his work he shows something of the great painter's affection for landscape—and indeed affection for friendly, warm, plump, pink women (the cinema has not often spoken up for plump, pink women). And the film he has based on *A Country Excursion* recreates the sunlight of a family outing to the country and a fleeting encounter. The mother (yes, a plump woman) is sensually excited by the ogling attentions of one of two young men on holiday by the river; the daughter, forgetting her dismal fiancé, timidly yields to the gentle approach of the other holidaymaker; and it is all over, romance, sunlight, everything; back to the family shop, back to that caricature of a lover who is to be her husband. Renoir suggests the hours of happiness in sensuous images—the orchard, the girl on the swing; he warns of the inevitable ending in the rainstorm which sweeps over the river, bending the reeds and shattering the polished face of the water. It is the counterpart of the Chekhov story—not love but the momentary reflection of love. I cannot think that the film is less a work of the imagination than its original.

As I see it, then, there are the writers who resist translation to the cinema, such as Dickens, and the writers such as Chekhov and Guy de Maupassant who, though working before the cinema was born, or at any rate in its infancy, seem ready to enter into a kind of partnership with the screen. And one must not forget those authors—not the kind of classic with whom I have up to now been concerned—who by the very nature of their work encourage the taking of liberties. Perhaps if one were to come unprepared on Mary Wollstonecraft Shelley's *Frankenstein* one would be startled by its progeny, poor sad monsters of the screen; but the charnel-house theme invites imitators. Bram Stoker, writing three-quarters of a century ago, might well be taken aback to find his *Dracula* not only so popular but so Protean: *Son of Dracula*, *Brides of Dracula* and all the rest of the descendants, a dozen and more, of the gifted Transylvanian Count. But then Bram Stoker brought myth to fiction, and myth cannot be expected to die. Even the figure of Sherlock Holmes has suffered a kind of degradation; I was deeply affronted when during the war he took part in a number of adventures alien from his habit—*Sherlock Holmes in Washington, Sherlock Holmes and The Secret Weapon*. Still, one has to admit that in general the basic character of the great man remained unaltered. Recently there was even an act of homage when the distinguished American director Billy Wilder gave us an affectionate and admiring pastiche called *The Private Life of Sherlock Holmes*. Perhaps we live in a borrower's age. The cinema borrows not only from Conan Doyle, it borrows from Henry James, and the other day gave us in *The Nightcomers* a prelude to *The Turn of the Screw*.

Sometimes, though, in borrowing it does not merely re-shape, it improves, it intensifies, it elevates. Most anarchic and disturbing of major film directors, Luis Buñuel fastens on a novel by Joseph Kessel about a young, happily married woman who takes to spending her afternoons in a brothel. Before the war, when *Belle de Jour* was published, it may have seemed mildly audacious. Today its study of the heroine's secret impulses strike one as superficial. But Buñuel has transformed the narrative into a dazzling complex of erotic and masochistic fantasies. The central narrative idea apart, there is scarcely anything left of Kessel; everything else is Buñuel surrealism, Buñuel black comedy, Buñuel undermining of the bases of conventional morality. At the last you are left uncertain of the line between reality and dream, uncertain what to believe and what to accept simply as an appalling, hilarious joke. I can find few parallels for such a gulf between a book and a film by a great director.

On the contrary, with contemporary fiction the relationship between the author of the novel or the play and the maker of the film grows closer; the original writer is consulted, perhaps collaborates on the script. Sometimes a modern novelist has an affinity with the screen. Graham Greene has written for the cinema, often in partnership with the director Carol Reed; the collaboration gave us *The Third Man* and *The Fallen Idol*. Mr. Greene was himself once a film critic; and reading his collected reviews puts us all in our places. The number of contemporary writers who complain of their treatment by the cinema dwindles; L. P. Hartley showed no dissatisfaction with the film of *The Go-Between*, and indeed it delicately held the sense of summer and heat and the innocence of the boy shuttlecocked, in a society outside his comprehension, between two lovers and two classes.

In the end, I suppose, we are thrown back on the problem not which books, or which plays, or which stories the cinema can embrace but which areas of experience it can encompass. Invite it to re-create the opening pages of *A Tale of Two Cities*—'It was the best of times, it was the worst of times'—and it is lost; that is a passage for words, and words alone. Ask it to introduce Maupassant's *Une Vie* and it responds with exquisite images: two girls, one in faint rose, one in luminous yellow run through flowers to pale sands and peacock sea—and here words on a page are at a loss. The cinema can give you the Joad family in *The Grapes of Wrath* leaving their home for ever; but it could never attempt the last, marvellous phrase of *The Arrow of Gold*. Perhaps (if I may for a minute forget *The Lady With the Little Dog*), it is at its best when it is on its own, carrying no responsibility to literature and the printed word; think of one of its masterpieces, think of *Citizen Kane*. And now I begin to feel guilty of treachery, a betrayal of the cinema in treating it as a translator of printed fiction and drama; for if it tries to be no more than that it is false to itself. It can be a partner to both fiction or drama. One must beware of looking on it as a servant. For the cinema is nobody's slave—not even the slave of literature.

FLAUBERT AND THE ART OF
THE SHORT STORY

By A. W. RAITT, M.A., D.PHIL., F.R.S.L.

(*Read 17 May, 1973*)

Joanna Richardson, M.A., F.R.S.L., in the Chair

PARADOXICAL as it may seem, it is by no means self-evident
that the greatest novelists make the greatest short-story writers,
still less that the greatest short-story writers can convert
themselves into even moderately successful novelists. H. E.
Bates has said of the short stories produced by eminent
nineteenth-century novelists like Thackeray and Meredith that
'they recall too often the dish hashed up from the left-overs of
the joint'; while on the other side, novels composed by masters
of the short story such as Hoffmann, Mérimée and Maupassant
tend to give the impression of an imperfectly joined mosaic of
independent episodes. Indeed, many expert practitioners of the
short-story form either never attempted to write a novel or
never managed to complete one—one thinks of Poe, Nerval,
Chekhov or Katherine Mansfield. The broad vision, the grand
design, the gift for synthesis required by the novel are not often
combined in the one mind with that ability for terse concentration, for the selection of significant detail, for the distillation
of meaning and emotion from a single action which are essential
for excellence in the shorter form. Only a handful of the
outstanding composers of narrative fiction have attained equal
mastery of both genres: Balzac, Turgeniev, Joyce and, perhaps
supreme among them, Gustave Flaubert.

Flaubert's case is moreover unusual in that, unlike the other
authors who have demonstrated comparable adeptness in
handling the two forms, he came to the short story through the
novel rather than the other way round. Balzac, Turgeniev and
Joyce had all established their reputation as short-story writers
before winning even greater fame as novelists. Flaubert on the
other hand, though as a schoolboy he wrote many tales in
imitation of the Romantics (borrowing not only the subject but
even the title of Mérimée's *Mateo Falcone*), began his public
career with *Madame Bovary* and thereafter, apart from occasional
misguided forays into the theatre, wrote nothing but novels

until he was in his fifties. There is no evidence that in the intervening period he ever contemplated turning his hand to the short story, and in the end it was largely accident that caused him to take it up in the 1870s and to produce that incomparable set of three masterpieces, his last completed work, which appeared under the title *Trois Contes* in 1877. The sequence of events is plain: half-way through the composition of his fascinating but impossibly ambitious *Bouvard et Pécuchet*, Flaubert's world was shattered when he had to sacrifice the whole of his fortune to save his niece and her husband from bankruptcy. Already exhausted by the almost unbelievable efforts he had expended on *Bouvard et Pécuchet*, saddened by a series of bereavements, discouraged by the invariably hostile and uncomprehending reception given to his novels, he so far lost confidence in himself that he despaired of ever being able to write again. It was in those unpromising circumstances that after several weeks of impotence he finally decided to experiment with the shorter form, 'to pass the time and to see if I can still write a sentence—which I doubt'. The result was *La Légende de Saint Julien l'Hospitalier*, a subject he had had at the back of his mind for many years and which he now managed to put on paper. The success of this exercise encouraged him to go on to *Un Cœur simple*, the story of a simple Norman serving-woman which he had likewise first conceived long before, and then to add *Hérodias*, his account of the beheading of St. John the Baptist, in order to make a volume of respectable size. That short stories written in conditions of such depression and discouragement by a man in his late fifties who had never hitherto taken seriously any narrative form other than the full-scale novel should turn out to be among the supreme examples of their kind seems little short of miraculous. It is the circumstances which made this near-miracle possible that I propose to look at today.

Perhaps the first point to be made is that in many ways Flaubert's three tales are unique, and that their aims and methods are quite unlike those of the vast majority of short stories. Traditionally, at least until writers like Chekhov proved that a short story does not necessarily consist of a complete and well-rounded plot, the short story has been the favourite vehicle of the *raconteur*, of the man adept at retailing anecdotes. Flaubert on the other hand was singularly impatient, in his maturity, with the whole idea of story-telling. His disdain for narration as such gives him a hankering after the unrealizable ideal of 'a book about nothing', and inspired an extraordinary tirade noted in the Goncourt journals:

I don't give a damn about the story, the plot of a novel. When I am writing a novel, my idea is to render a colour, a tonality. For instance, in my novel about Carthage, I want to do something purple. In *Madame Bovary*, my one thought was to produce a grey coloration, the damp, rotting colour of the existence of woodlice. I was so little concerned with the story that had to be put in it that a few days before I began writing the book, I had imagined *Madame Bovary* quite differently.

Plot for Flaubert is then subservient to the need to produce a particular impression, definable in terms of colour as here, but perhaps also as a shape, as a texture, or as a rhythmic experience (whence, at least in part, the primordial importance he accorded to style).

This is as true of his short stories as it is of his novels. There is in them no hint of that dramatic and suspenseful unfolding of a striking anecdote which characterizes so many nineteenth-century short stories; no unexpected twist in the action, no surprise ending, not even the single salient incident around which most writers like to construct their tales. *Un Cœur simple* indeed relates the life-story of a humble maidservant to whom nothing exciting ever happens, and though the events of *Hérodias* are intensely dramatic, one may wonder how far Flaubert really is concerned with giving his version of the execution of John the Baptist when one realizes that the work appears to have originated with the idea of writing a novel of political life under the Second Empire entitled *Monsieur le Préfet*. Even with *Saint Julien l'Hospitalier*, which has the strongest and clearest story-line of any of the three tales, it is difficult to avoid the feeling that Flaubert's real preoccupation is less with the medieval hagiographical legend for its own sake than for the unspoken themes that lie behind it and that first attracted him to it. Of course, this is not to deny the meticulous attention which Flaubert pays to the mechanism of plot or the art with which he organizes and gradates dramatic effects. But he does stand alone among the writers of his time in regarding anecdote not as the essential object of a short story but as one element among many which combine to form a finished artefact the value and significance of which far transcend the sequence of events which it recounts.

One reason why anecdote in Flaubert's short stories loses the primacy it tends to have elsewhere lies no doubt in the remarkable process of maturation which the subjects of all three tales underwent. In the nineteenth century, the short story was closely associated with journalism, and there is no doubt that pressure to meet newspaper deadlines or desire to exploit a highly profitable vein sometimes led even the most conscientious artists to make use of subjects which had not properly ripened in their minds—some of Maupassant's greatest tales only acquired their ultimate quality when he had reworked at leisure ideas first published in almost skeletal form and had added to them the flesh and blood of human reality. Likewise, necessity often forced Villiers de l'Isle-Adam hurriedly to write up a story that he would have preferred to mull over much longer. With Flaubert, not only is such haste unthinkable, but when he did decide to write his tales, he chose subjects which had begun to take shape in his imagination years and even decades before. The story of St. Julien had probably first come to his notice in 1835; in 1846 he had talked of one day writing his own version of it; he had done some desultory reading for it in 1856; but it was only in 1875 that he eventually committed it to paper. Adumbrations of *Un Cœur simple* likewise go back to his childhood: a character much like Félicité figures in a tale he wrote at the age of fifteen, and, strange as it seems, was almost taken as the heroine of *Madame Bovary*: 'the first idea I had was to make her into a virgin, living in the depths of the country, growing old in misery, and ending in the last stages of mysticism and imagined passion'. Only *Hérodias* seems to be a relatively new subject, but even there he had been taking notes for it five years previously, as well as reflecting on *Monsieur le Préfet* from which its underlying theme derives. The result is that the subjects had all acquired an extraordinary richness of texture and resonance through this long process of evolution: the alluvial deposits left by years of meditation, experience and feeling have given them a depth of fertility almost unequalled in the short story.

This quality of complex profundity is enhanced by the fact that Flaubert never makes explicit—perhaps not even to himself—precisely what significance he attaches to the subjects. Whereas many short-story writers either deliberately underline what sense the reader is meant to extract from a tale, or else so arrange its elements that the intended effect is clear and unambiguous, in the *Trois Contes* Flaubert points no morals, drops no hints, suggests no interpretations. Events are related with detachment; comment is eschewed. This is not only a function of that celebrated impersonality on which Flaubert laid such stress, and which is perhaps more perfectly realized in these tales than in any of his other works. It arises also from the singularly concrete quality of his imagination, which leads him from the outset to conceive a narrative in the uniquely individual terms of material reality, of particular people in a particular setting and in a particular light. Unlike for instance Zola, who for the most part worked by defining a general idea or plan and then constructing characters and incidents to flesh it out, Flaubert sees plot, character and structure as an indivisible unity, endowed from the start with a presence and an individuality of its own, from which all abstract and generalizing elements are rigorously banished. Thus it is that before writing a word of *Hérodias* he exclaimed to a friend: 'I can *see* (clearly, as I can see the Seine) the surface of the Dead Sea, sparkling in the sun. Herod and his wife are on a balcony from which one looks out over the golden tiles of the Temple.' So too with Félicité, whose existence and surroundings are visualized with a meticulous and single-minded intensity that immerses us in the very stuff of her being. In the notes and drafts for *Un Cœur simple* one can see Flaubert living Félicité's life with a passionate empathy that makes every detail, every incident vividly present for him. Many of the details and incidents in the end are sacrificed and do not appear in the finished text, but both those that survive and those that are removed help to convey a rare sense of a unique, irreplaceable personality, as strongly individuated as any living being. One is struck too, even in the manuscripts, by Flaubert's absolute refusal to identify Félicité's characteristics in the vocabulary of psychological typology or emotional analysis, which would detract from the uniqueness of her experience. The stories thus acquire a three-dimensional quality extremely rare in works so short, and at the same time provide the reader with the sense of a reality which, like that of life itself, is meaningful, but with a meaning that cannot be circumscribed in abstract formulas or precise definitions.

A consequence of this mode of creation is that an entirely new role devolves upon description. In most short stories, as in most pre-Flaubert novels, descriptive passages serve essentially as background, as the stage setting in which the characters will appear to act out their parts. For Flaubert description serves a different purpose. It is an integral part of the whole experience of the figures whom he writes about and into whose lives we enter. Flaubert sees that no feeling and no event can exist in the abstract; it is always inseparably associated with the physical circumstances in which it occurred and can only be evoked by reference to them. Look for instance at the scene where Félicité arrives at the convent after the death of her beloved Virginie: 'Félicité went up to the second floor. From the doorway of the room, she could see Virginie lying on her back, her hands clasped together, her mouth open, her head tilted back under a black crucifix that leant over her, her face whiter than the curtains that hung motionless on either side. Mme Aubain was clinging to the foot of the bed and sobbing desperately. The Mother Superior stood to the right. Three candlesticks on the chest of drawers added touches of red to the scene, and fog was whitening the windows. Some nuns led Mme Aubain away.'[1] Though this is one of the emotive climaxes of the tale, Flaubert says nothing at all about Félicité's feelings; instead, he puts us in her position so that we see the picture as she saw it and would recall it. The moment in time is fixed indelibly by visual means; the emotions are implied, not stated in what would inevitably have tended to be undifferentiated abstractions—grief, sorrow or whatever. The same technique, adapted to suit the aesthetic and technical postulates of each tale, is used throughout the book. It is perhaps most apparent in *Un Cœur simple* because the point of view is almost always Félicité's and because the simple-minded Félicité, devoid of any capacity for intellectual abstraction, lives above all in her physical contacts with the outside world (that is what motivates and justifies her consoling deathbed vision, in which she *sees* her parrot as the Holy Ghost receiving her into heaven). But it is also strongly and vitally present in *St. Julien,* where the whole narration of the saint's life is an implicit allusion to a stained glass window, as is made clear by the last sentence: 'And that is the story of St. Julian Hospitator, more or less as it is depicted on a stained-glass window in a church in my part of the world.' As for *Hérodias*, it contains a wealth of descriptive writing which communicates a stifling sense of the remorseless pressure of a physical milieu. Each tale thus creates its own imaginative world which the reader can move into and inhabit as with perhaps no other short stories.

All this implies that, just as Flaubert assigns a special and unusual function to description in his stories, so he does with detail. It is customary for short-story writers to impose unity

---

[1] The quotations from *Trois Contes* are in the excellent translation by the late Robert Baldick, F.R.S.L.

on their works by focusing the reader's attention on one or two significant details, carefully selected for their evocative power or their symbolic overtones—one thinks of the vase in Mérimeé's *Le Vase étrusque*, which acts as both the cause and the emblem of Saint-Clair's jealousy, or in Vigny's *Laurette*, of the sinister red seal on the letter which is the hero's death warrant. Flaubert does not operate in that way in the *Trois Contes*. Even where a particular object is given especial prominence and fulfils a central function in the tale, as with Félicité's parrot, it remains only one among a whole variety of similar objects—in the remarkable passage in which he catalogues the contents of Félicité's room, Flaubert only arrives at the parrot after having listed scores of other possessions, many of them known to us from previous episodes in the story. Likewise in *Hérodias*, though the last sentence narrows the focus right down to the severed head borne by the disciples—'as it was very heavy, they each carried it in turn'—the preceding scene, in which the head is passed around the various guests at the feast, has already reduced it to the status of only one object among the many depicted in the story. This relative fullness of detail gives the tales a texture more akin to that of novels than is usual in short stories, and obviates that feeling of somewhat contrived bareness that lesser authors may inadvertently convey in their desire for concision.

It is indeed noteworthy that each of the *Trois Contes* contains much more material, and material of a much more diverse kind, than authors usually think it wise to include in works of such brevity. *Un Cœur simple* and *La Légende de Saint Julien l'Hospitalier* both consist of biographies which follow their protagonists through from birth to death, instead of relying on the much more common short-story technique of using a single incident to illuminate a whole life, as Maupassant so frequently and so brilliantly does. *Hérodias*, it is true, compresses its events into twenty-four hours, but they form a pattern of such intricate complexity, involving so many different named characters, that many readers, from Flaubert's time to the present day, have found it confused, difficult, and obscure. It may well be that it was Flaubert's long and undivided pre-occupation with the novel that led him to take such apparently unwieldy subjects when he eventually turned to the shorter form; but the fact remains that, with the possible exception of *Hérodias*, the challenge is magnificently met and overcome. How has Flaubert carried off this exceptional feat?

Here it becomes necessary to differentiate between the three stories and to analyse each of them separately to see how in each case Flaubert has solved the problems posed by his choice of material. In *Un Cœur simple*, the main difficulty arises from the necessity of providing a sense of unity and a forward-moving impetus in the long and uneventful time-span of Félicité's existence, a difficulty increased by the obstacles in the way of involving the reader in the experiences of an illiterate and inarticulate serving-woman who communicates with nobody and who never reflects on her own situation. The key to Flaubert's resolution of the difficulty is to be found above all in his astonishingly subtle use of *style indirect libre*, the free use of the imperfect tense to convey the thoughts and feelings of a character without resorting either to direct quotation or to accurately reported speech. It is of course one of the outstanding features of Flaubert's style throughout his prose fiction, but nowhere is it put to better or more consistent use than in *Un Cœur simple*, where its peculiar advantage is that it enables the author, almost from one end of the story to the other, to be simultaneously within his character and outside her. The unity of point of view is thus more rigorously preserved than anywhere else in Flaubert's fiction, yet without limiting his expressive resources to the exiguous vocabulary and rudimentary mental equipment of his heroine. Consider for instance the sentence describing the end of Félicité's long and anxious wait for the return of her stuffed parrot: 'At last he arrived— looking quite magnificent, perched on a branch screwed into a mahogany base, one foot in the air, his head cocked to one side, and biting a nut which the taxidermist, out of a love of the grandiose, had gilded.' The perceptions contained in the sentence are not explicitly referred to Félicité, but one notices that the supposed magnificence of the bird must represent her reaction to it while the absurdity of the golden nut stuck in its beak, implied only by the exaggeratedly climactic rhythm of the phrase, cannot be. The repeated use of this technique throughout the tale entails very careful handling of language so as to prevent the reader sensing any dichotomy between author and character: the sentences are relatively short and simple in structure, the images are few, unobtrusive and mostly culled from the world of nature and domesticity with which Félicité was familiar, the vocabulary is restrained and homely. A delicate balance is thus consistently maintained which enables Flaubert to create a unified work of art out of what at first blush might have seemed diffuse and unpromising material.

The problems of *La Légende de Saint Julien l'Hospitalier* are different. The legend with its contrasting scenes of hunting, parricide, expiation and apotheosis, has a dramatic energy of its own, which Flaubert exploits to the full. But he has added a further, unexpected dimension to it by viewing it not only as a story to be told in its own right, but also as a re-creation of medieval art. Hippolyte Taine perceptively remarked to him: '*Julien* is very true, but it is the world *imagined* by the Middle Ages, and not the Middle Ages themselves; which is what you intended, since you wanted to produce the effect of a stained glass window; that effect is there; the pursuit of Julien by the animals, the leper, it's all the pure ideal of the twelfth century.' The effect is created from the start by all manner of barely perceptible touches: an almost fairy-tale vagueness in the setting ('Julian's father and mother lived in a castle in the middle of a forest, on the slope of a hill'), a naïve exaggeration in the descriptions ('lands so hot that men's hair caught fire like torches in the burning sun'), a discreet use of archaic terms and old-fashioned constructions, a matter-of-fact acceptance of the supernatural, more ornate and colourful imagery, a deliberate stylization of the secondary characters. Avoiding the pitfalls of pastiche on the one hand and incongruity on the other, Flaubert has produced a highly original and successful medieval tonality in the language and presentation of *Saint Julien*. This achievement is all the more striking in that, despite appearances, the legend is more than an artificially ingenious aesthetic exercise. Running through it is not only a carefully and convincingly motivated study of a man in the grip of an uncontrollable blood lust, but also a disturbing complex of underlying themes interrelating cruelty, eroticism, guilt, and atonement through self-immolation. These undertones are all the more effective for remaining unspoken. The *Légende* is not only one of Flaubert's most elusively enigmatic works; it is also, in its very detachment and distance, one of his most personal.

In *Hérodias*, Flaubert himself was painfully aware of the intractability of the material on which he had decided to work. Repeated complaints in his letters bear witness to the struggle he had to render it artistically viable: 'the problem is, so far as possible to do without indispensable explanations'; . . . 'I have landed myself with a little piece that is anything but easy, because of the explanations the French reader needs. To produce something clear and lively out of such complex elements presents gigantic difficulties.' With his customary scrupulousness, he had spent two months reading everything he could find on the death of John the Baptist and its historical, political, religious, social, and racial background—at least thirty books and articles zealously studied and annotated—and Taine claimed that *Hérodias* had taught him more about the origins of Christianity than the whole of Renan's vast work on the subject. But it is undeniable that Flaubert has sought to include in the story more information than the average reader could reasonably be expected to assimilate—even Taine himself misread one passage where concision had led to ambiguity.

But one should beware of the facile assumption that in *Hérodias* Flaubert is simply a historian who knows too much to make himself comprehensible to the profane. *Hérodias* is not a historical reconstruction, though it may look like one. As Flaubert once declared, 'I consider technical details, precise information, in short the historical and exact side of things, to be very secondary. Above all else, I am seeking for beauty, which my fellow-writers don't much care about.' That this principle is applied here is shown by the numerous historical anachronisms and mis-statements in *Hérodias*, which arise not from carelessness but from a conscious decision to sacrifice factual accuracy to a higher truth. This means that ultimately the reader has no need to remember the mass of detail about people, places, sects, parties, beliefs, politics and so forth which is so profusely supplied in the first part of the story. What Flaubert wants to do is to build up a vast network of pressures bearing down on the Tetrarch Herod and weighing on the administrative decision, fraught with consequences, that he has to take about the life or death of his prisoner Iaokanann (John the Baptist). It is of little moment if the reader cannot follow the daunting complexity of the factors involved, since Herod cannot either; and in the end, when Salome dances, everyone forgets them, united only in the lust for the girl: 'And the nomads inured to abstinence, the Roman soldiers skilled in debauchery, the avaricious publicans, and the old priests soured by controversy all sat there with their nostrils distended, quivering with desire.' The decision to execute Iaokanann is wrung from Herod by a frenzy of animal desire, not by a rational consideration of the rights and wrongs of the case. It is in this that as Flaubert says in a letter, Herod 'was a real prefect' and that *Hérodias* is revealed as the projected novel *Monsieur le Préfet* in another guise. And the totally unforeseen ironic consequence of Herod's decision, as we realize from the concluding tableau of the disciples bearing away the prophet's head, symbol of his message, is the spread of Christianity.

Once one reads the story in that light, it becomes clear that the detail in it, the multiplicity of characters, the constantly shifting point of view are essentially subservient to an impressionistic purpose, and the sensitive reader will understand that, implicitly, *Hérodias* constitutes a devastatingly misanthropic and pessimistic comment on the way humanity conducts its affairs. There is, in other words, a hidden design which justifies and binds together the apparently multifarious threads of which the story is composed. The unity of focus in *Hérodias* is less easy to grasp than in the other two tales; perhaps even it is less perfectly realized, at least on the surface. But its presence gives the tale its real strength and originality.

It appears then evident that, however belated and unorthodox Flaubert's cultivation of the short-story form may have been, he was intensely alive to the peculiar problems it posed and enormously skilful in solving them. That he did succeed so magnificently is in no small measure due to the seriousness with which he set about his task. He may have started *Saint Julien* as a less demanding enterprise than the crushing burden of *Bouvard et Pécuchet*, but that was above all a matter of scale. Once he had decided to write these tales, he treated them with precisely the same scrupulous conscientiousness, precisely the same attention to detail, precisely the same fanatical care over style as he brought to his novels. It has been calculated that, proportionately to their length, *Trois Contes* were written just as slowly and with just as much difficulty as *Madame Bovary*, and the piles of manuscript material in Paris and Rouen, recently published in full for the first time, demonstrate how meticulously he documented himself (even for *Un Cœur simple*, on parrots, on pneumonia, on religious processions), how thoroughly he thought out the plan of each tale, how many times he was prepared to draft and redraft their expression. There is no hint of that slightly supercilious attitude to the short-story genre one occasionally detects in great novelists, and which may be responsible for the casualness with which someone like Zola tossed off the most disastrously inept little tales. Whether Flaubert ever in so many words tried to distinguish the principles of short-story writing from those of the novelist's art is open to doubt, but it is certain that in practice he did not make the mistake of treating the tale as a truncated or embryo novel. Formally, the *Trois Contes* have an unmistakable identity of their own—or perhaps it would be fairer to say three separate identities, since there is no question of a threefold application of the same formula—and though they could certainly not have been written without the years of meditation and experience Flaubert had devoted to the novel, they show that the lessons of those years had been used flexibly and sensitively to fit in with the conditions of a different form.

It remains to ask what the *Trois Contes* add to the corpus of Flaubert's works. Would our image of the writer be the same if he had never written them, or do they contain something new and irreplaceable, not to be found elsewhere in his writings? It is as well first of all to dissipate one possible misunderstanding, namely that each of the *Trois Contes* is a pendant to a major work of which it repeats the effects in miniature. In this way, *Un Cœur simple* has been claimed to follow *Madame Bovary*; *La Légende de Saint Julien*, *La Tentation de Saint Antoine*; and *Hérodias*, *Salammbô*. It is true enough that, as we have already seen, there is a close relation between the genesis of the subject of *Un Cœur simple* and that of *Madame Bovary*. It is true too that Flaubert himself was worried about the resemblance between *Hérodias* and *Salammbô*: 'I'm afraid of reverting to the effects produced by *Salammbô*, since my characters belong to the same race, and it's more or less the same setting.' But apart from the theme of sainthood and asceticism, there is little to connect *Saint Julien* with *Saint Antoine*, the one intimately dependent on its medieval atmosphere, the other set in a desert in the ancient world. Even with the other two tales, the similarity with the novels is more apparent than real. After expressing his fears about *Hérodias* and *Salammbô*, Flaubert goes on: 'however, I trust that this criticism, which people will no doubt level at me, will be unjustified', and so indeed it proves to be. *Salammbô* is basically concerned with dark and mysterious themes linking mysticism and carnality, eroticism and death; *Hérodias* is a bitterly ironic comment on human frailty and animality. Indeed, one might be tempted to argue that *Salammbô* in that respect is closer to *Saint Julien*, and that the pessimism of *Hérodias* relates it more cogently to *La Tentation* or even to *Bouvard et Pécuchet*. As for *Un Cœur simple*, despite the unmistakable features which it has in common with *Madame Bovary*, especially in its evocation of the Norman countryside and the humdrum monotony of provincial life, Flaubert was in no doubt that it marked a new departure in his art, and it is worth considering in what ways this is so.

Though the idea of the story is old, *Un Cœur simple* was in the end committed to paper in response to a sort of challenge from George Sand. For years, she and Flaubert had been conducting a running argument about impersonality in literature, and in 1875 she had finally got under his skin by accusing him of wilfully depressing his readers: 'you create desolation', she said. Flaubert defended himself by claiming that he had no desire to desolate people but that he could not change his eyes: he had to tell the truth about life as he saw it. But clearly the reproach rankled, and *Un Cœur simple* was begun as an attempt to show George Sand that, without departing from his canons of impersonality or falsifying his view of the world, he could nevertheless write a work the effect of which would be consoling. 'You will see from my story of *Un Cœur simple*, where you will recognize your direct influence, that I'm not as stubborn as you think. I believe you'll approve of the moral tendency of the work, or rather of its human undertones.' Unfortunately, George Sand never read it, as she died before it was finished, so we do not know how she would have reacted to it. But it is clear that, to please her, Flaubert was trying to do something he had never done before, and this is what gives *Un Cœur simple* its unique quality and makes it for many readers Flaubert's greatest work.

In order to achieve his end, Flaubert has centred the work on a character who is wholly admirable and who leads her life in a way that renders her proof against the buffetings of fate. Félicité's whole existence is dominated by the selfless love she feels for others—her suitor Théodore, the children, Paul and Virginie, her haughty employer Mme Aubain, marching soldiers, cholera victims, a dying old man, and finally her parrot. Each of these objects of her love is successively taken from her, and the progression is one of ever-diminishing human contact, from people close to her to strangers, then to an animal, and finally, after Loulou the parrot's death, to a stuffed relic, a thing. But because she never expects anything in return, this apparently catastrophic decline into total solitude does not destroy her as a similar decline destroys Emma Bovary. On the contrary, her virtue is rewarded by the tranquillity of her soul (to use the words noted by Flaubert in the margin of one of the manuscripts), and she dies in peace with the beatific vision of the parrot receiving her into heaven. The contrast with Emma's hideous death-bed vision of the blind beggar looming up over her is exemplary. Emma has lived only for herself and the result is disaster: Félicité (so aptly named, and without irony) has lived entirely for and in others, and the result is the only life-story in Flaubert's works, with the possible exception of *Saint Julien*, that carries its own justification within itself and that provides its protagonist with an unshakable inner equilibrium. It is as if she had heeded the advice proffered by Flaubert to his niece while he was working on the story: 'so far as possible, one should always concentrate on things outside oneself; otherwise one drowns in a sea of sadness. Take the word of an old man rich in experience.' This is the solution momentarily and accidentally adopted by Frédéric Moreau, the hero of *L'Éducation sentimentale*, when with amateurish enthusiasm he studies to become a historical writer; in the most revealing aside in the book, Flaubert says: 'As he immersed himself in the personality of others, he forgot his own, which is perhaps the only way not to suffer from it.'

Un Cœur simple thus reverses the customary pattern of the world depicted in Flaubert's fiction, where idealism is trampled underfoot and mediocrity triumphs. Here, without commentary or sentimentality, we are shown a character who finds serenity and equilibrium amid adversity, and who dies happy, as the work moves to a soberly majestic conclusion. Here lies the 'consolation' Flaubert wished to demonstrate to George Sand; but here too is the same harshly clear-sighted vision of life everywhere present in his works. Viewed objectively, Félicité's life is a long succession of disappointments, hardships, misunderstandings, and the world in which she moves is as grim and bleak as any Flaubert depicts. But because he constantly refuses to step outside her and judge her situation from above, and because she has none of the introspective intelligence which would enable her to see it for herself, as Emma Bovary eventually sees the reality of her position, she keeps her faith undimmed to the end. The vision of the celestial parrot may be an illusion, but it is an illusion which remains intact, and the reader is induced to acquiesce in it and to share in the sense of beatitude which descends on her. This tenderness towards Félicité and the extraordinary tact of feeling which permits Flaubert to preserve his customary pessimistic outlook while producing a work which is morally uplifting, make *Un Cœur simple* fundamentally different from everything else he wrote.

The *Trois Contes* do then in their different ways add something of their own to the greatness of Flaubert, not least because he has used the short narrative form to say some of the things most important to him. In both theme and technique he has treated the short story as of equal stature with the novel. This is indeed what gives these tales their peculiar and lonely eminence in the history of the nineteenth-century short story. For they do not fit easily into the story of the evolution of the genre, since Flaubert has largely ignored the lessons of great predecessors like Mérimée and has developed his own concept of the form from his experience as a novelist. Likewise, subsequent practitioners, even his disciple and close friend Maupassant, have not seen fit to follow his example in this field. The *Trois Contes*, by their complexity, their density, the subtlety and power of their themes, the sense they convey of a depth and breadth of life extending far beyond their apparently restricted confines, stand alone among French and even among world short stories.

QUEEN VICTORIA AS AN AUTHOR

By GILES ST. AUBYN, F.R.S.L.

(Read 27 April 1972)

The Countess of Longford, F.R.S.L., in the Chair

I PROPOSE to start with a confession, in the hope that even the gravest fault may be mitigated by its candid avowal. My principal qualification for addressing you this evening is the ruthless way in which I have plundered Lady Longford's book: a treasure-trove for the light-fingered. After I have shared the spoils with you, I believe you will be obliged to concede that I am a discriminating thief. Furthermore, the aptness of my subject may help excuse the crime, for there could hardly be a more appropriate theme for this Royal Society of Literature, than Queen Victoria as an author.

The oddest thing about Disraeli's remark, 'We authors, Ma'am', is not so much that it is apocryphal—indeed it is stamped with the hallmark of truth—but that it is regarded as evidence of his insincerity. Admittedly, Disraeli delighted in flattery, and 'when it came to royalty he laid it on with a trowel'. But in describing the Queen as an author, he was recognizing a fact, not indulging his fancy. Whatever the merits of her style, and there is much to be said for its unadorned vigour, she devoted a large part of her day to reading and writing. The sheer quantity of paper Queen Victoria covered in sixty years entitles her to be regarded as an author. She wrote on average about two thousand five hundred words a day, achieving a total of sixty million in the course of her reign. If she had been a novelist, her complete works would have run into seven hundred volumes, published at the rate of one a month. In the archives at Broadlands there are twelve hundred letters written to Palmerston in her own hand, and he was only one of twenty or more ministers with whom she corresponded at length. She wrote to the Princess Royal at least twice a week, and sometimes twice a day, for over forty years—from the time her daughter left England as a young bride, until the dawn of the twentieth century. While writing to Vicky in Berlin, she was exchanging letters with Uncle Leopold in Brussels, keeping a massive journal, and maintaining her official correspondence.

Few of the Queen's letters were printed until after her death,
but during her lifetime she published her Highland journals.
It was only with the greatest difficulty that candid friends persuaded her not to print a book about John Brown. General
Grey's *Early Years of the Prince Consort* made use of her letters and
diaries, and was written under her direction. All five volumes of
Sir Theodore Martin's life of Prince Albert were meticulously
supervised by her Majesty. Not only did she help him to collect
and arrange his material, but again and again, as Mr. Fulford
has noticed, 'her easy, vivid style springs out at the reader from
the more sober language' of her husband's official biographer.

Despite the speed at which Queen Victoria wrote, and the
vehemence of her utterance, she hardly ever left a word out by
mistake. If her punctuation was inclined to be emphatic, her
spelling was almost infallible. 'I must tell you', she wrote to
Vicky, with a hint of relish, 'that you have mis-spelt some words
several times . . . you wrote in two letters appeal and appreciate
each with one p.' After the birth of the future Kaiser, his mother
received a further rebuke: 'I am glad baby is installed (not
enstalled as you wrote it) in his new rooms.'

Five English sovereigns have either published books or had
books attributed to them. In 1521 Henry VIII wrote *A Defence
of the Seven Sacraments* and presented it to Leo X. It went
through twenty editions during the King's lifetime, provoked
a rejoinder from Luther, who dismissed Henry as a 'miserable
scribbler', and won him the title of 'Defender of the Faith'.
Luther hinted that Edward Lee was principally responsible
for the book, a suspicion not dispelled when Lee was made
a bishop. Others attributed authorship to Sir Thomas More.
James I wrote several theological tracts, pamphlets on politics,
and *A Counterblaste to Tobacco*. His style was erudite but for-
bidding, and taxed the loyalty of the most obsequious subject.
Charles I was alleged to have written *Eikon Basilike* which ran
into forty-seven editions, and inspired Milton's *Eikonoklastes*.
Only Queen Victoria and her great grandson, the Duke of
Windsor, ventured upon autobiography.

The Queen's two books were instant best sellers. *Leaves from
the Journal of Our Life in the Highlands* sold more copies than
Browning's *The Ring and the Book*, Wilkie Collins's *The Moonstone*,
or Mrs. Allcott's *Little Women*, all of which came out in 1868.
More Leaves was published in 1884, and overshadowed both
Spencer's *Man Against the State* and the English edition of
Huckleberry Finn. The Queen was thrilled by her success.

'From all and every side,' she told Vicky triumphantly, 'letters flow in, saying how much more than ever I shall be loved, now that I am understood, and clamouring for the cheap edition for the poor—which will be ordered at once. Eighteen thousand copies were sold in a week.' A couple of months later, she sent the Crown Princess a 2s. 6d. edition of the book, describing it as 'nicely got up'. It had already sold thirty-five thousand copies, and fifteen thousand more were being printed. It was little wonder that the Queen's head was turned. Mary Ponsonby noted with amusement 'the literary line the Queen has taken up since her book was published'.

After the Prince Consort's death, Queen Victoria determined that nobody should ever be allowed to forget her beloved husband. The Albert Hall, the Albert Bridge, the Albert Memorial, preserved his precious name. During the bitter months after his fatal illness, his disconsolate widow resolved to commit her recollections of him to paper, while every detail was agonizingly fresh in her mind: the sound of his voice, the very words he had used, every gesture, every look. In May 1863 she wrote to Vicky outlining her plan, and asking for help:

You know I have been trying to put down an exact account of our happy life, as a picture of it, as well as all I can remember beloved Papa said. Well I began with the life at Windsor, beginning in October and going on, and I have got down to the description of Christmas and the end of the year . . . It would be a very great help to me if you would describe New Year's Day as it used to be . . . beginning with you children standing in our room waiting for us with drawings and wishes; Grandmama at breakfast, then you children performing something, or a tableau, and your playing and reciting, and in the evening generally a concert or performance with orchestra . . . In short, try and help me a little bit, and put down any picture of darling Papa's manner—as I am very anxious to get everything I can together for my book (which will belong to you all after my death) and for the private life General Grey is working at.

At first, the Queen intended what she was writing for her own family only, but Arthur Helps persuaded her to share the book with her subjects. Helps came to her notice when in 1860 he was appointed Clerk to the Privy Council. He was an enchanting conversationalist, a friend of Dickens, Kingsley, and Carlyle, and a well-known author in his own right. In 1862 he edited *Speeches and Addresses of the Prince Consort*, and prefaced the work with so handsome an appreciation that thereafter the Queen was convinced that he possessed exceptional discernment.

During one of his official visits to Balmoral, he was given a glimpse of the Highland journal. Such was the interest he expressed in it, that it 'occurred to her Majesty that the extracts, referring as they did to some of the happiest hours of her life, might be made into a book, to be printed privately, for presentation to members of the Royal Family and her Majesty's intimate friends'. A tussle ensued between those, like Helps, who thought the book should be given to the world, and the Queen, who disclaimed 'any skill whatever in authorship' and 'felt reluctant to publish anything written by herself'. In view of the frigid way in which the book was received by almost all her family, it was unfortunate that none of them was consulted while she wrestled with such misgivings. But Helps finally persuaded her to publish, respectfully pointing out 'that, if printed at all, some portions of the volume might find their way into the public journals. It would, therefore,' he thought 'be better at once to place the volume within reach of her Majesty's subjects' who would be gratified to know 'how her rare moments of leisure were passed in her Highland house'.

The Queen gave Vicky her own account of her reasons for printing the journal.

It was so much liked [she explained] that I was begged to allow it to be published—the good Dean of Windsor amongst other wise and kind people saying it would, from its simplicity and the kindly feelings expressed to those below us, do so much good. I therefore consented—cutting out some of the more familiar descriptions and being subjected by Mr. Helps and others to a very severe scrutiny of style and grammar . . . Mr. Helps has written a very pretty preface to it. . . . No one can conceive the trouble of printing a book, and the mistakes which are endless.

Helps's role as literary adviser to the Queen might have dismayed a lesser man, for her Majesty was more accustomed to deliver rebukes than to receive them. But nothing daunted he chided her over grammar, waged war on colloquial phrases, and lectured her for mis-using the word 'so'. On one occasion when he had retired to bed for the day, she sent him an engaging note. 'The Queen', it read, 'is so grieved (perhaps Mr. Helps will scold her for that so!) to hear of Mr. Helps feeling so ill today.' In her private letters she sometimes employed the most improbable slang. 'Now goodbye and God bless you,' she once wrote to Vicky, 'and as Papa says, "keep up your pecker".'

The Highland journal, unlike the chapter on the rupee which Miss Prism omitted, could hardly be called 'sensational'.

But then the home life of the Queen was mostly uneventful. Her descriptions of it, however, are not without interest or touches of unconscious humour. 'I sat down to sketch, and poor Vicky, unfortunately, seated herself on a wasp's nest, and was much stung. Donald Stewart rescued her, for I could not, being myself too much alarmed. Albert joined us in twenty minutes. . . . What a delightful day!' That was not, as might be supposed, a parody by Max Beerbohm, but a genuine extract.

One longer quotation must suffice to give the flavour of the book. In September 1861 the Queen and Prince Albert embarked on what she called the 'Second Great Expedition', during which they stayed one night incognito in a village inn. Her account of this simple event is endearingly characteristic. It shows her capacity to enjoy life to the full, it reveals her meticulous if undiscriminating eye for detail, and it illustrates her talent for telling a plain tale:

At a quarter-past seven o'clock we reached the small quiet town, or rather village, of Fettercairn, for it was very small—not a creature stirring, and we got out at the quiet little inn, 'Ramsay Arms', quite unobserved, and went at once upstairs. There was a very nice drawing-room, and next to it, a dining-room, both very clean and tidy—then to the left our bedroom, which was excessively small, but also very clean and neat . . . Alice had a nice room, the same size as ours; then came a mere morsel of one, in which Albert dressed; and then came Lady Churchill's bedroom, just beyond; Louis and General Grey had rooms in an hotel, called 'The Temperance Hotel', opposite. We dined at eight; a very nice, clean, good dinner. Grant and Brown waited. They were rather nervous, but General Grey and Lady Churchill carved, and they had only to change the plates, which Brown soon got into the way of doing. A little girl of the house came in to help—but Grant turned her round to prevent her looking at us! The landlord and landlady knew who we were, but *no one else* except the coachman, and they kept the secret admirably.

The evening being bright and moonlight and very still, we all went out, and walked through the whole village, where not a creature moved—through the principal little square, in the middle of which was a sort of pillar or tarn cross on steps, and Louis read, by the light of the moon, a proclamation for collections of charities which was stuck on it. We walked on along a lane a short way, hearing nothing whatever—not a leaf moving—but the distant barking of a dog! Suddenly we heard a drum and fifes! We were greatly alarmed fearing we had been recognized, but Louis and General Grey, who went back, saw nothing whatever. Still, as we walked slowly back, we heard the noise from time to time—and when we reached the inn door, we stopped, and saw six men march up with fifes and a drum (not a creature taking any notice of them), go down the street, and back again. Grant and Brown had no idea what it could be. Albert asked the little maid, and the answer was, 'It's just a band', and that it walked about in this way twice a week. How odd! It went on playing some time after we got home. We sat till half-past ten working, and Albert reading—and then retired to rest.

Got to sleep after two or three o'clock. The morning was dull and close, and misty with a little rain; hardly anyone stirring; but a few people at their work. A traveller had arrived at night, and wanted to come up into the dining-room, which is the 'commercial traveller's room', and they had difficulty in telling him he could *not* stop there. He joined Grant and Brown at their tea, and on his asking, 'What's the matter here?' Grant answered, 'Its a wedding party from Aberdeen.'

More often than not, the journal was reviewed generously and most critics seemed to accept its author's contention that it would help to reform fashionable Society by portraying the simple life of the Court. The Queen attributed the book's success to the happy picture it gave of her family and her highland friendships. Disraeli congratulated Helps with un-restrained enthusiasm. 'Its vein', he declared, 'is so innocent and vivid, happy in picture, and touched with what I ever think is the characteristic of our Royal mistress—grace. There is a freshness and fragrance about the book like the heather amid which it was written.'

The Duke of Cambridge, the Queen's first cousin, shared the family view of the journal. 'The Queen's book is out of print,' he wrote to his wife, Louisa, 'but it is a pity, I think, that it was ever published.' He had not by then received a signed copy and consequently felt neglected. But when one eventually reached him, he was highly delighted. 'The Queen sent me the book', he told Louisa, 'handsomely bound and with a very pretty inscription in the fly-leaf. "To dear George in re-collection of his dear friend and cousin, from his affectionate cousin." Very nice I think, don't you?'

Vicky received the Highland journal coldly. Like her mother she was devastatingly honest, and the fact that she said so little, suggests reservations she preferred to keep to herself. 'You have never said a word about my poor little highland book —my only book', complained the Queen, eager to elicit some reaction. 'I had hoped that you and Fritz would have liked it.' Perhaps Vicky still was stung by that callous reference to the wasp's nest. In subsequent letters the Queen reverts to the success of her journal, without provoking a flicker of response.

'Newspapers shower in,' she announced, 'the poorest, simplest, full of the most touching and affectionate expressions. The kind and proper feeling towards the poor and the servants, will I hope do good, for it is very much needed in England among the higher classes.' No answer! Only her own children, so it seemed, refused to acknowledge her triumph. But the Queen was too pained by Vicky's silence to leave it at that. 'I have such beautiful and touching letters,' she told her, 'from people whom I don't know, or have ever heard of—all about my little book, but I send you none, as you seem to take so little interest in it. Here everyone is so full of gratitude and loyal affection, saying it is not to be told the good it will do the throne, and as an example to the higher classes.' At last Vicky replied, but without offering her own opinion. 'I do not know', she said, 'why you should think I am indifferent about the appearance of your book . . . whatever concerns you and our home is of vital importance and greatest interest, not of indifference. The Article in the Edinburgh Review (which I always take in and read regularly) I thought very kind and well worded.'

In February 1884 the Queen published *More Leaves from a Journal of a Life in the Highlands*. The first volume had com-memorated 'the dear memory of him who made the life of the writer bright and happy'. The second volume was gratefully dedicated 'To my loyal Highlanders, and especially to the memory of my devoted personal attendant, and faithful friend, John Brown'. Once more the Queen's book was acclaimed, and once more her family disapproved. The Prince of Wales discussed his mother's journal with the old Duchess of Cam-bridge, and told her that he was 'indignant and disgusted at the Queen's publishing it'. But then, he said, there was 'no one to prevent her committing such acts of insanity'. According to Lady Geraldine Somerset, the Duchess's lady-in-waiting, the book was miserably trivial, and written in 'bad, vulgar English'. Helps, whose own literary style Ruskin had admired, died before the second volume was finished, but evidently his efforts to purify the Queen's English had not proved entirely success-ful. The Prince of Wales having read an advance copy of the book, was bold enough to express 'grave doubts' whether his mother's 'private life should be, as it were, exposed to the world'. He begged the Queen to restrict the book to her family and friends. 'You will, dearest Mama, I am afraid not agree in this, but I hold very strong views on the subject.' So, however, did the Queen, and she told him that if she took his advice, the

book would be confined to the very members of Society least
likely to appreciate 'simple records'. 'I know', she added, by
way of clinching the argument, 'that the publication of my
first book did me more good than anything else.' The Prince
returned to the fray with a new grievance, little expecting the
pounding to which he exposed himself. Some friends had told
him how surprised they had been to find no mention of him in
the journal. So he wrote to his mother, suggesting that she
should include an account of his recent visit to Balmoral in the
next edition of *More Leaves*. He ended this unfortunate letter
by saying that as the book was 'finding its way all over the
world, it might create surprise that the name of your eldest son
never occurred in it. . . .' The Queen at once wrote back asking
whether he had actually read the book, 'or whether he had
commissioned "so called friends", who were bent upon making
mischief, to read it on his behalf'. If he had been kind enough to
read the book carefully, he must have seen that his name was,
in fact, mentioned on pages 1, 5, 8, 331, and 378. It would, the
Queen concluded, have been mentioned more often, had he not
refused so many invitations to Balmoral.

Not long after Brown died, Queen Victoria invited Martin
to write a memoir of 'her best and truest friend'. Sir Theodore
declined the commission, lamely pleading his wife's ill-health.
After rejecting a number of other possible biographers, the
Queen decided to write the life herself. She wrestled for months
with the manuscript, and when it was finished, gave it to
Ponsonby to read. If Sir Henry had a fault it was moral
cowardice. He hesitated to oppose the Queen directly, even
when he was convinced that she was wrong. Behind her back
he could be most amusing about her, but to her face he was
ever her humble servant. He did his best to suggest that it would
be a disaster if Brown's life ever found its way into print, but
somehow the force of his objection became lost in a maze of
diplomacy. The memoir, he said, was 'invested with a degree of
interest which must be felt by all who knew Brown'. But he,
nevertheless, ventured to doubt 'whether this record of your
majesty's innermost and most sacred feelings should be made
public to the world. There are passages which would be mis-
understood if read by strangers, and there are expressions
which will attract remarks of an unfavourable nature towards
those who are praised . . . Sir Henry cannot help fearing that
the feeling created by such a publication would become most
distressing and painful to the Queen.'

Although Ponsonby never came nearer to defying her Majesty than on this occasion, it is improbable that his unsupported effort would have succeeded. It was left to Randall Davidson, then Dean of Windsor, to prevent her publishing and being damned. He told her that there were some among the humbler classes who had proved themselves unworthy of her confidence, and had indulged in impertinent criticism of her latest book. 'These facts,' he said, 'which are, I fear, beyond dispute, do not in any way detract from the respectful sympathy with which all the better natures among your Majesty's subjects accept this volume from your Majesty's hands—but the facts remain and give a special point to words which I venture to quote from the letter your Majesty was good enough to write me a few weeks ago: "the sacredness of deep grief may be desecrated by unholy hands".' The Queen expressed outraged surprise at Davidson's views. He wrote again, dwelling on the inappropriateness of publication, and announcing 'that he would feel bound to take every means of persuading her, if possible, to desist'. This time he was asked to withdraw his remarks, or, at the very least, to apologize for the pain his letter had given. Davidson replied that he was naturally distressed to have grieved the Queen, but felt bound to 'reiterate his view as to what was right'. For a fortnight he neither saw nor heard from the Queen, but was left in no doubt by third parties that her silence signified displeasure. Then, at last, he was summoned. The proposed book was never mentioned, but all was sunshine and the Dean was forgiven. 'In the long run', he remarked afterwards, 'her sound common sense always prevailed. . . . My belief is that she liked and trusted best those who occasionally incurred her wrath, provided she had reason to think their motive good.' Discretion triumphed, Brown's memoir was set aside, and the world is a sadder place for its loss.

Although relatively few of Queen Victoria's letters were published in her lifetime, apart from those quoted in Prince Albert's official biography, they constitute her major legacy to literature and are, perhaps, the more readable because never intended for publication. Raymond Mortimer has described them as among the most enjoyable letters in English; 'compared with those', he says, 'of Lady Bessborough or of Mrs. Carlyle, they are artless in the extreme; but the simplicity of her style reflects the shining simplicity of her character. She could not have dissembled, even if she had so wished—which she never did. Few letter-writers have revealed their feelings more openly. Her pen made everything personal and expressive, the phrasing, the changes from the third person to the first, the exclamation-marks, the indefatigable underlinings.' She cheerfully wrote letters under the most trying circumstances. 'I beg you to excuse this being so badly written', she implored her Uncle Leopold, 'but my feet are being rubbed, and as I have got the box on which I am writing on my knee, it is not easy to write quite straight—but you must not think my hand trembles.'

The great merit of the Queen's letters, the simple language in which they were written, owed more to art than to accident. In an age in which ornament ran riot, she rejected a decorated style, even finding fault with dear Lord Beaconsfield's novels. 'Finished reading Conningsby', she wrote at the time of the Congress of Berlin, 'a very remarkable, strange book. There are some beautiful sentiments in it, and some very striking opinions, a sort of democratic conservatism. . . . The story is strange, and the language too stilted and unnatural.' The celebrated advice with which Fowler begins his book aptly describes the Queen's English. 'Anyone who wishes to become a good writer should endeavour, before he allows himself to be tempted by the more showy qualities, to be direct, simple, brief, vigorous and lucid.' Queen Victoria certainly practised what Fowler preached. When, for example, it was suggested by the Prussian royal family that Vicky's wedding should take place in Berlin, the Queen wrote to the Foreign Secretary:

It would be well if Lord Clarendon would tell Lord Bloomfield [the ambassador to Prussia] not to entertain the possibility of such a question as the Princess Royal's marriage taking place at Berlin. The Queen never could consent to it, both for public and private reasons, and the assumption of it being too much for a Prince Royal of Prussia to come over to marry the Princess Royal of Great Britain in England, is too absurd, to say the least . . . Whatever may be the usual practices of Prussian Princes, it is not every day that one marries the eldest daughter of the Queen of England. The question must therefore be considered as settled and closed . . .

What could be more 'direct, simple, brief, vigorous and lucid'?

The variety of people to whom the Queen wrote letters rivalled the diversity of subjects they embraced. Not all her correspondence was conducted with celebrities, like King Leopold, Lord Tennyson, or Mrs. Lincoln. Lord Kilmarnock wrote to Ponsonby, saying that he was horrified to discover that one of his little boys 'had written to her Majesty and the servant had stupidly posted the letter . . . In case it should reach its destination I hope you will explain the circumstances, and express our profound regret that such a thing should have happened. I find he had been reading a story in which the hero had taken a similar step, which I suppose put the idea into his head. I hope his extreme youth may be accepted as an excuse for its indiscretion.' 'Pray tell Lord Kilmarnock', Sir Henry was instructed, 'that the Queen was delighted with the letter of his little boy, as nothing pleases her more than the artless kindness of innocent children. She has written him an answer, and has posted it to him.'

The Queen's despair at Albert's death—a constant theme of hundreds of letters—partly arose from her total dependence upon his help and advice. 'How I, who leant on him for all and everything—without whom I did nothing, moved not a finger, arranged not a print or photograph, didn't put on a gown or a bonnet if he didn't approve of it, shall be able to go on, to live, to move, to help myself in difficult moments? How I shall long to ask his advice. The day—the night (above all the night) is too sad and weary.' The Queen recognized that the melancholy tone of much of what she wrote was more gratifying to the writer than the reader. Soon after the Prince Consort's death, Vicky lent her mother a bundle of his letters. 'How admirable, how perfect all are!' the Queen wrote back. 'How every word he wrote was like his precious self . . . Poor dear Child, when I read them, how did I feel what you had lost! What wretched, stupid letters mine are, in comparison to those! No one ever wrote as he did! How you must be bored and grieved by mine which are merely the outpouring of the deepest woe and agony.'

Nearly forty years on, Albert was still missed and still remembered, but when the Queen returned to Balmoral for the first time after his death, she was overwhelmed by grief. All around her were Albert's possessions and everything reminded her of her lost happiness. Tortured by yearning, she wrote to her old friend, Queen Augusta of Prussia, Vicky's mother-in-law: 'In this house I see him, hear him, search for him everywhere! . . . When I am in the open and everything is as it used to be, I cannot believe that my beloved Albert is not out shooting as usual—then every evening comes the terrible return home, which is so agonizing to me! The house is empty, quiet, desolate! Where is he? . . . I could go mad from the desire and longing.'

Although the Queen's letters, bordered in black, were written in melancholy tones, the funeral note was not the only one struck. The Queen never forgot that she ruled half the world, and her majestic utterances echoed round the courts and chancelleries of Europe. Fond as she was of the Kaiser, her first grandson, she did not conceal his shortcomings from him. When, in 1900, he ventured to interfere in South Africa, she wrote to the British Ambassador in Berlin: 'Please convey to the Emperor that my whole nation is with me in a fixed determination to see this War through without intervention. The time for and the terms of peace must be left to our decision.' Lord Salisbury was delighted with such firmness, and the Prince of Wales's Secretary described it as 'worthy of Elizabeth'.

Queen Victoria never allowed her children to forget that she was their sovereign as well as their mother. Vicky objected to Louise's engagement to Lord Lorne, believing her sister should only marry a Prince. She said as much in a letter home and was denounced, by return of post, as shameful, undutiful, heartless, and disrespectful. 'When your parent and your Sovereign settles a thing . . . opposition for mere selfish and personal objects is monstrous.' Although the Queen's family bore the brunt of offended Majesty, Gladstone knew what it was to vex her.

The Queen [she once told him] trusts Mr. Gladstone is recovering from the hoarseness with which he has been troubled for so many months, and takes this opportunity of expressing a hope that he will spare himself from speaking in public meetings for some time to come. [If he finds it absolutely necessary to do so] he might do a great service by dissociating himself entirely from the extreme set of visionaries who excite the people's hopes and aspirations by promises of what is impracticable or dangerous. There are many persons who are becoming greatly alarmed by the destructive doctrines which are taught, and would welcome warmly any word of Mr. Gladstone's, which affirmed that liberalism is not Socialism and that progress does not mean revolution.

The Queen's mind was essentially practical, and her letters are full of instructions and advice. When Vicky took up residence in Prussia, her mother repeatedly expressed the fear that she would grow 'sickly and old' before she was twenty, because of the hot, stuffy rooms and theatres of Berlin. The Queen's indifference to cold was dreaded by her guests, few of whom shared her tastes in matters of climate. Even when she was well over seventy, she would drive through rain and snow in an open carriage, expecting her ladies-in-waiting, often little younger than herself, to enjoy being soaked to the skin. When the mood of evangelical fervour was upon her, nobody preached more eloquently the merits of bracing fresh air. Indeed, her formula for long life consisted of draughts and laxatives. 'Now dear,' she told Vicky, 'you should positively get someone to be answerable that the rooms, and still more the passages, are never above a certain and given temperature, having (as we have everywhere) thermometers hanging up in them, and by keeping to that—the stoves ought to be kept out or let up. And then the windows should be opened regularly three times a day, or oftener, if it is warmer.'

As a 'soldier's daughter', the Queen always took a special interest in military matters, and insisted upon signing the commission of every officer: a fatiguing imposition, but one which, nevertheless, symbolized the Sovereign's supremacy. No detail was too minute to escape her attention. 'The Queen', she wrote in 1856, 'returns the drawings for the "Victoria Cross". She has marked the one she approves with an x. She thinks, however, that it might be a trifle smaller. The motto would be better "For Valour", than "For the Brave", as this would lead to the inference that only those are deemed brave who have got the "Victoria Cross".'

The murders of Jack the Ripper provoked a frenzy of regal exhortation. When the news of yet another victim reached Balmoral, she telegraphed to Lord Salisbury, insisting that 'This new most ghastly murder shows the absolute necessity for some very decided action. All these courts must be lit, and our detectives improved. They are not what they should be. You promised, when the first murder took place, to consult with your colleagues about it.' If the Prime Minister had been discovered surreptitiously lurking in the alleys of Whitechapel, he could hardly have been made to look more guilty, although, in fact, he had issued a proclamation that very day from Downing Street, offering a free pardon 'to anyone who should give evidence as to the recent murder, except the actual perpetrator of the crime'. But the Queen was far from satisfied, and drafted a letter to the Home Secretary, expressing her misgivings about the effectiveness of police inquiries, and offering a number of practical suggestions.

No doubt [she wrote] the recent murders were committed in circumstances which made detection very difficult; still the Queen thinks that, in the small area where these horrible crimes have been perpetrated, a great number of detectives might be employed, and that every possible suggestion might be carefully examined and, if practicable, followed. Have the cattle boats and passenger boats

been examined? Has any investigation been made as to the number
of single men occupying rooms to themselves? The murderer's
clothes must be saturated with blood and must be kept somewhere.
Is there sufficient surveillance at night? These are some of the
questions that occur to the Queen on reading the accounts of this
horrible crime.

It seems not impossible that they had also occurred to the
harassed police in charge of the case.

Fortunately, the Queen's letters were more often concerned
with family news than mass murder. Like other mothers, the
Queen assumed that everyone shared her interest in children
and welcomed anecdotes about them. Whether Uncle Leopold
really wanted to know that Vicky had been kicked off her pony,
seeing that she was 'not the least hurt' is matter for conjecture,
but he probably was amused to learn of Alfred's wilful reck-
lessness. 'Alfred', so his niece wrote, 'whom you will recollect
I told you was so terribly heedless, and entirely indifferent to
all punishment, tumbled downstairs last week. He was not
seriously hurt at all, and quite well the next morning, only with
a terrible black, green, and yellow face, and very much swelled.
He might have been killed; he is always bent upon self-
destruction, and one hardly knows what to do, for he don't
mind being hurt, or scolded, or punished; and the very next
morning he tried to go down the stairs leaning over the
banisters just as he had done when he fell.'

The Queen is dead, but in the pages of her letters and
journals, Long lives the Queen. Every word she wrote provides
a self-portrait. All the strange contradictions of her character
tumble from her pages. She wrote abruptly and she was abrupt.
Her sentences have the staccato cadence of a telegram. At
one moment, she is angry, stubborn, and imperious; at the
next, touching and affectionate: every inch a Queen and
yet engagingly humble. The style was the woman. Randall
Davidson regarded common sense as her crowning virtue, a
quality which Dr. Johnson raised to the point of genius. Queen
Victoria was no philosopher, unlike Prince Albert or Vicky.
She had probably never heard of Bishop Berkeley, or the
idealist theory of knowledge. But had she done so, she too might
have stubbed her toe on a stone and growled: 'I refute it thus.'
When Sir John Cowell warned her that the church was in
danger, threatened apparently by Mr. Courtenay's insistence
upon describing himself as 'the Reverend and honourable', she
remained as calm as the doldrums. 'It is a matter', she said, 'of

perfect indifference to the Queen what he is called', and thus resolved the crisis. E. F. Benson, in *As We Were*, describes Queen Victoria as 'a woman of peerless common sense; her common sense which is a rare gift at any time, amounted to genius . . . She looked very steadily with her rather prominent blue eyes on every situation that presented itself, and made up her mind as to what was the level-headed and the sensible thing to do . . . Common sense poured out from her, grey and strong, like the waters of the Amazon.'

Perhaps the most formidable characteristic of Queen Victoria was her devastating regard for truth. She said exactly what she meant, and was, if anything, downright to a fault. Bright said she was the most truthful woman he had ever met. 'If old mama has a virtue,' she once told Vicky, 'it is of truth and the absence of all flattery.' Princess Marie Louise recalls in her memoirs being dumped as a child at Windsor, while her mother, Princess Helena, wintered abroad. 'Children very well,' telegraphed the Queen to the South of France, 'but poor Louise very ugly.' When, later in life, Princess Louise reproached her Grandmother, and said, 'Grandmama, how could you send such an unkind telegram?' she replied, 'My dear child, it was only the Truth!' The Queen was equally brutal about her own children. Leopold she described as 'tall, but holds himself worse than ever, and is a very common looking child, very plain in face, but an oddity'. Of her son and heir she wrote: 'I think him very dull; his three brothers are so amusing and communicative.' Only those disposed to follow Alice into Wonderland should accuse Queen Victoria of hypocrisy.

Vicky inherited the Queen's fearless honesty, and when mother and daughter disagreed their candour was awesome. Tennyson wrote some lines for 'the dear Mausoleum' in memory of the Duchess of Kent. The Queen thought them very beautiful, but Vicky did not. I will quote the verse so that you may choose sides in the dispute.

> Long as the heart beats life within her breast,
> Thy child will bless thee, guardian mother mild,
> And far away thy memory will be blessed
> By children of the children of thy child.

'I am afraid', wrote Vicky, 'I did not quite like the lines under dear Grandmama's statue. I thought them not quite simple enough—not one of Tennyson's happiest efforts, but that is a matter of taste and I suppose you all like them very much.' 'I am sorry and surprised', replied the Queen, 'you do not like the lines. I admire them very much, especially that line "Thy child will bless thee, guardian mother mild".' So there it was, but at least each knew what the other thought.

The Queen's hatred of artificiality and sham perhaps encouraged her to overvalue the simplicity and directness of John Brown, 'the child of nature' as Ponsonby christened him. 'Her reliance on him is partly explained by the simple truth that she was refreshed by an human being untrammelled by convention or the wish to please.' What was once said of Macaulay applied with greater force to his sovereign. He 'sought truth, not as she should be sought, devoutly, tentatively, and with the air of one touching a sacred garment, but clutching her by the hair, and dragging her about in a kind of boisterous triumph, a prisoner of war and not a goddess.'

The more one immerses oneself in Queen Victoria's letters and journals, the more one is forced to admire their author. Even Lytton Strachey, although determined to mock, ended by marvelling. As Tennyson remarked to his wife, 'One felt that no false thing could stand before her.' Perhaps that was why Mr. Gladstone sometimes shuffled uneasily in the presence. At her best, she was capable of delightful expressions. Count Bernstorff, the Prussian Ambassador in London, was one of those people as quick to take offence as to give it. The Queen, describing a diplomatic reception in 1865, remarked: 'The good Bernstorffs were, as usual, in a sort of porcupine condition which is so odious.'

Let the Queen have the last word, as she was wont to do. When she sent the Poet Laureate a copy of *More Leaves from a Journal of a Life in the Highlands* she enclosed a note with it describing herself as 'a very humble and unpretending author'. But she added that she hoped the book had one merit: 'its simplicity and truthfulness'. In so saying, as always, she went straight to the root of the matter, for these were precisely the qualities which adorned every moment she reigned and every sentence she wrote.

MARIE STOPES MEMORIAL LECTURE

This lecture is in memory of Dr. Marie Carmichael
Stopes, scientist and author, a Fellow of this Society
from 1913 until 1958. She was an active friend and
benefactor of the Society and this lecture has been
founded in gratitude

ROSE MACAULAY IN HER WRITINGS

By CONSTANCE BABINGTON SMITH, M.B.E., F.R.S.L.

(Read 1 March 1973)

Mary Stocks, Ll.D., Litt.D., F.R.S.L., in the Chair

ROSE MACAULAY once said she wished that she could be
remembered as a poet, rather than as a novelist. She must
have known this could never happen, but the remark gives us
a useful clue as we set out to discover her in and through her
writings. Though of course she was much more than a novelist
and a poet; she was essayist, commentator, scholar, historian,
and Christian apologist too (in her own very original way).

In and through Rose's writings we can find the writer, the
born writer, but beyond this we can find the person, the
paradoxical, contradictory person, justly renowned for her
clear-thinking and gaiety and humour, but also possessed of
a melancholy side, an emotional feminine side.

First however I would like to make it clear that I lay no claim
whatever to being a literary critic. It is not for me to try and
'place' Rose, or to analyse her works. But having known her
well towards the end of her life, and having just spent some
years working on her biography, I can truly say that I am close
to her.

Writing was second nature to Rose, and she gave herself
to it. In her talk she was reticent, for behind the chatter she was
shy and sensitive. But in the written word she reveals herself,
in her novels obliquely, in her non-fiction directly and em-
phatically, with the wit that one of her friends has called
'*un*common sense neatly phrased'. Her essays are a good

starting-point. Here, for instance, are some of her views on 'The Problems of a Writer's Life', taken from a piece she wrote in the 1920s, the time when she first adopted this sort of idiom:

The primary trouble in the life of a writer is, of course, writing. Any form of work is insufferably tedious, and this not least (though assuredly not most, either). You cannot get round or escape this trouble; in the long run, defer it as you may, you will find that the law at last holds good: writers must write. They need not write much, and very certainly they need not write well, but a little something now and then they must produce, or they will, as the phrase is, go under . . . It is a frightful compulsion. For what has to be produced is not mere agreeable dalliance, mere unthinking self-expression, with the pen instead of the tongue as medium as was the pleasant habit of our childhood [in Rose's case it was not only in childhood]. Over all that we now write hangs the shadow of an awful doom: it will Come Out . . . and make a fool of us . . . But there is a worse doom than getting into print—not getting into print . . . This is one of the heaviest troubles of a writer's life . . . He does not demand to be a best-seller; he does not even demand a *succès d'estime*, or that critics should call him clever. But he would like, he would very much like, just to be in print, so that those could read him who might so wish . . . A writer's life is not all jam. Besides the primary and heavy trouble of having to write, and the even heavier trouble of being neither published nor paid, his life contains many incidental griefs. He will, for instance, be asked from time to time to do things which he has no taste for, such as . . . contributing to anthologies, speaking in public, writing articles on subjects which do not please him. He may, in his folly, if the date . . . is a long way ahead, say he will do it, supposing that the time will never come, for he may die first, or the world may end, or it may please God to take him to whom he has made the promise. But alas! none of these things occur; inevitably the date does come.

Most of Rose's early essays were in this jaunty vein: or should one perhaps call them *articles* rather than essays? Between the wars they often enlivened the *Daily Express*, the *Daily Mail* and the *Evening Standard*, as well as the *New Statesman* and the *Spectator* (for quite a time in the thirties she took on 'Marginal Comments'). Few people realize how much she contributed to the daily and weekly press; if a full bibliography of her writings were to be compiled the catalogue of her journalism would be formidable. Later on, she also reviewed many books for the *Times Literary Supplement* and the *Observer*, and wrote occasionally for the *Listener*, *Time and Tide*, *Encounter*, *Horizon*, the *Cornhill*, and—in her pacifist days—*Peace News*.

I think one reason why Rose enjoyed writing for the press was that she had a great relish for argument and intellectual controversy, especially if the issues were ethical ones. Long ago, as an undergraduate at Somerville, she had been an ardent debater. She had the quickness, and the zest for a lively fray, of one who as a young woman was a keen hockey player. Most of us who remember Rose remember her as she was in her seventies, pale, fragile, angular, pencil-thin. We forget that in her youth she had shared in the same rough games and sports as her brothers. The tomboy who had assumed that she would one day grow up 'to be a man' retained a virility of mind—so we can see in her writings—that excluded all sentimentality. One of the things that attracted Gerald O'Donovan to her, so a friend of his remembered him saying, was that she had 'a mind like a man'. And it is interesting that *Potterism*, her first novel to show the full impact of his influence (*What Not* was a transitional book), bears the following dedication: 'To the unsentimental precisians in thought, who have, on this confused, inaccurate, and emotional planet, no fit habitation.'

Potterism, Rose's satire on the popular press, which was published in 1920, was her first best-seller, though by no means of course her first novel. In fact it was her tenth; her earliest, *Abbots Verney*, had appeared in 1906. Such a steady output might suggest that writing novels was from the start an inner compulsion for Rose, but this was not so. Rather it had proved an easy means, ready to hand, of escape from the tedium of living at home. We know this from letters she wrote to a Somerville friend.

Some of her early novels were well received, and one of them, *The Lee Shore*, won a literary prize. But none of this gave Rose any confidence in herself as a writer of fiction. Even after *Potterism*, and all the subsequent successes of her 'middle period', she still insisted that she was not *really* a novelist. In 1934 when Frank Swinnerton told her that he planned to include a section on her in his book *The Georgian Literary Scene*, she replied to him: 'Must there be a section about me? You see, I never feel like a novelist at all, and would much rather only my essays, or literary books, or even verse, were discussed . . . I think my own novels so bad (as novels) that no one could think them worse. All I am interested in when I write them is the style—the mere English, the cadences, etc. . . . and sometimes when I make a joke. As stories, and as characterizations, they bore me to death.' To another friend, Daniel George, she once wrote: 'I never dare to read my novels once they are published . . . Perhaps when I am very old I shall dare, and shall feel no more responsibility for them . . . Till then I shall refrain.'

And it was not only in private letters, but in print, that Rose spoke out on this matter. In her essay on Writing—on the Pleasure of Writing—in *Personal Pleasures*, she was frank about her shortcomings as a novelist, as she herself saw them. She also confessed to her heartfelt passion for language and words. *Personal Pleasures* was published in 1935, when Rose had just returned to topical satire with *Going Abroad*, after her love for the seventeenth century and its language had blossomed in *They Were Defeated*.

Heaven never, I think, destined me for a storyteller, and stories are the form of literary activity which gives me the least pleasure. I am one of the world's least efficient novelists; I cannot invent good stories, or care what becomes of the people of whom I write. I have heard novelists complain that their characters run away with their books and do what they like with them. This must be somewhat disconcerting, like driving an omnibus whose steering-wheel, accelerator and brake are liable to be seized by the passengers. My passengers know their places, and that they are there to afford me the art and pleasure of driving . . . I have heard of novelists who say that, while they are creating a novel, the people in it are ever with them, accompanying them on walks, for all I know on drives (though this must be distracting in traffic), to the bath, to bed itself. This must be a terrible experience; rather than allow the people in my novels to worry me like that, I should give up writing novels altogether. No; my people are retiring, elusive, and apt not to come even when I require them. I do not blame them. They no doubt wish that they were the slaves of a more ardent novelist, who would permit them to live with her. To be regarded as of less importance than the etymology and development of the meanest word in the dictionary must be galling.

And so we come to words, those precious gems of queer shapes and gay colours, sharp angles and soft contours, shades of meaning laid one over the other down history, so that for those far back one must delve among the lost and lovely litter that strews the centuries . . . Words, living and ghostly, the quick and the dead, crowd and jostle the otherwise too empty corridors of my mind, to the exclusion, doubtless, of much else that should be there. How charmingly they flit before me, heavy laden with their honey like bees, yet light on the wing; slipping shadowy out from dusty corners, hiding once more, eluding my reach, pirouetting in the air above me, now too light, too quick, to be caught in my net, now floating down, like feathers, like snowflakes, to my hands.

They arrange themselves in the most elegant odd patterns; they sound the strangest sweet euphonious notes; they flute and sing and taber, and disappear, like apparitions, with a curious perfume and a most melodious twang. Or they abide my question; they offer their pedigrees for my inspection; I trace back their ancestry, noting their diverse uses, modes, offspring, kin, transformations, transplantations, somersaults, spellings, dignities, degradations . . . lines and phrases which have enambered them for ever, phrases and lines which they have themselves immortally enkindled. To move among this bright, strange, often fabulous herd of beings, to summon them at my will, to fasten them on to paper like flies, that they may decorate it, this is the pleasure of writing.

England, the pirate, has ransacked the countries of Europe for her speech; Greece, Rome, France, Germany, Scandinavia, have poured in tribute to her treasury, which shines and jingles with the most confused rich coinage in the world. To play with these mixed coins, to arrange them in juxtaposition, to entertain oneself with curious tropes, with meiosis . . . hyperbole, pleonasms, pedanticisms, to measure the words fitly to the thought, to be by turns bombastic, magniloquent, terse, flamboyant, minishing, to use Latinisms, Gallicisms, Hellenisms, Saxonisms, every ism in turn, to scatter our native riches like a spendthrift tossing gold—this is the pleasure of writing. It is this, rather than concern with relating of human beings, which can hold me thralled through a night, until, in the long street outside my high windows, the pale morning creeps, and the scavengers arrive with little carts to remove the last day's dust. It is dalliance with this pleasure that I promise myself when I think of work; it is, alas, dalliance with it that too often abets me in my day-long and easily accomplished business of keeping work at arm's length. For to hunt language, to swim lazily in those enchanted seas, peering at 'whatsoever time, or the heedless hand of blind chance, hath drawn from of old to this present in her huge drag-net, whether fish or seaweed, shells or shrubs, unpicked, unchosen' may well fill a day with such pleasure that to put pen to paper in the way of business, of getting on with some task in hand, seems too rude an interruption. Rather let me set down lines of verse, phrases of prose, experiments in rhythm and sound, images and pleasing devices, as they come into my mind, without relation to any larger work to be accomplished. Let me be an amateur of verse and prose, dealing in fragments only.

But . . . who will buy these fragments, unstrung, unset, without context or co-ordinated form? Who will buy the fish or seaweed, shells or shrubs, caught in my drag-net, scattered loosely like the twigs of white coral and the oyster shells with which Italian fisher lads pursue the foreigner, crying *Frutto del mare*? No one (heaven forgive readers and heaven help writers) desires such loose jetsam. They desire books. And, oh, God of literature and of achieved tasks, how incompetent do I feel adequately to produce these!

Rose's love of words leads us on very directly to her poetry. And to discover her in her poetry means first of all going back to her childhood. 'One has to write poetry (at least I always have)', she once told a friend, 'to express things that don't go into prose so easily; also, I like playing with metres and rhythm; it was, in childhood and youth, one of my forms of insobriety . . . I used to write a lot of poetry once; as a child it was my great outlet when things were almost too beautiful to bear.'

As a little girl in Italy, when her family lived on the Ligurian coast, her writing was intimately connected with her reading. Much of her time was of course spent playing with her brothers and sisters, in and out of the sea, but she often slipped away alone and sat in an olive tree up the hill, or in an ivy clump on top of the *orto* wall, reading and writing poetry—she doted on Browning and Tennyson, but most of all on Shelley—or steeping herself in stories of high adventure. And she herself once described the 'inner life' which her reading stimulated. This was in a broadcast called 'I speak for myself':

Yes . . . side by side with . . . [the] outer life . . . what is sometimes called the real life . . . runs another life, the inner life, equally real, the life of imagination and fantasy . . . In early childhood the mind is an open receptacle for anything poured into it. My mind was nourished always largely on literature. Myths, adventures, romantic tales of all kinds, were my mental food from infancy . . . Stories of Greek heroes and gods, of battles, voyages, desert islands, adventures in fairyland and in forests, by sea and by land, filled my mind, transformed me into an explorer, a sailor or soldier, a page in the tents of a prince, a knight fighting in a tournament, Perseus with winged heels . . . I would turn myself into a bird, like the Grand Vizier in my book of Indian fairy stories . . . and fly hither and thither from land to land. I crept on hands and knees through wild forests stalking Red Indians, or, caught by them, I bravely endured torture at the stake. I ran with Mowgli's wolf pack, leaped across great ravines, plunged into rivers pursued by wild dogs, rode my pony into battle against enemy spears. Needless to say, I showed, on all occasions, great courage and resource; I was praised for these qualities by captains and kings. I adventured in all lands; the plains of India knew me, the high snowy mountains, and the scorched desert where I lay parched with thirst. This grand romantic life ran on, while the ordinary little girl that I was went on her ordinary way, playing, doing lessons, climbing trees, bathing, canoeing, quarrelling, later applying herself in a rather half-hearted way to her studies. But it was more than a life; it was a world; a magic world; a key turned, a door swung back, and in one went. Sometimes the key would be poetry, sometimes music, sometimes a sweet smell, sometimes the sight of sudden beauty, a blue cove between rocks, a sunset, ponies cantering by, a lonely hillside . . . hot in the brooding noonday, frogs croaking in ponds beneath a summer moon. The world was suddenly magicked; it slid into an eerie dream. Its ecstasy possessed me utterly; after I had recovered my senses a little, I wrote poetry, the only vent for such dreams.

Alas! Only a couple of Rose's earliest poems have survived. But one of them, 'The Sea', won a poetry competition when she was in the sixth form at the Oxford High School and was published in the school magazine. Here is a taste of it:

> Sunny and calm and bright,
>   Ocean, great ocean,
> Lit with the sky's blue light,
>   Fathomless ocean!
> No movement stirs thy silent smiling deep,
> No playful breeze disturbs thy peaceful sleep,
>   But far on the distant land
> The ripples dance upon the yellow sand,
>   Ocean,
> Upon the shingly sand.
>
> Gloomy and dark and sad,
>   Ocean, wild ocean,
> Stormy and black and mad,
>   Terrible ocean!
> The wild waves thunder on the wind-swept shore,
> Toss angry crests, and surge and rush and roar,
>   Towering dark and high,
> Flinging their light spray to the angry sky,
>   Ocean,
> To the wild, sullen sky.

By the time Rose was in her mid-twenties, and then on through her thirties, she wrote quite a lot of poetry, and her verses, which often appeared in the *Saturday Westminster*, tended towards melancholy, nostalgia, and strange apprehensions, although a few were lively. One of the best known of them, 'Trinity Sunday', written when the Macaulays were living near Cambridge, combines these two contrasting tempers.

> As I walked in Petty Cury on Trinity Day,
> While the cuckoos in the fields did shout,
> Right through the city stole the breath of the may,
> And the scarlet doctors all about

Lifted up their heads to snuff at the breeze,
And forgot they were bound for Great St. Mary's
To listen to a sermon from the Master of Caius,
And 'How balmy', they said 'the air is!'

And balmy it was; and the sweet bells rocking
Shook it till it rent in two
And fell, a torn veil; and like maniacs mocking
The wild things from without peered through.

Wild things that swam in King's Parade
The days it was a marshy fen,
Through the rent veil they did sprawl and wade
Blind bog-beasts and Ugrian men

And the city was not. (For cities are wrought
Of the stuff of the world's live brain,
Cities are thin veils, woven of thought,
And thought, breaking, rends them in twain.)

And the fens were not. (For fens are dreams
Dreamt by a race long dead:
And the earth is naught, and the sun but seems:
And so those who know have said.)

So veil beyond veil illimitably lifted:
And I saw the world's naked face,
Before, reeling and baffled and blind, I drifted
Back within the bounds of space.

I have forgot the unforgettable
All of honey and milk the air is.
God send I do forget . . . The merry winds swell
In the scarlet gowns bound for St. Mary's.

The early stages of Rose's career as a poet are the stages she described so well in *Told by an Idiot*. She was very young for her age, and 'Imogen', the tomboyish romantic adolescent, has a great deal of Rose in her:

Imogen . . . wrote and published verse and prose. After all, it didn't matter what one wrote . . . Written words opened the door, that was all. Beyond the door lay the adventure, bright and still and eerily clear, like a dream . . . Why write of what should, instead, be lived? Nevertheless, one did write, and was, inexplicably, praised for it. Black marks on paper, scribbled and niggled and scrawled, and here and there the splendour and the joke and the dream broke through them, like sunshine flashing through prison bars, like music breaking through the written notes.

And then there is a moving passage telling of how Imogen's inspiration came to her:

Ecstasy descended on the wood; enchantment held it, saturating it with golden magic. Ants and little wood-beetles scuttled over Imogen's outstretched hands and bare, rough head. . . . She was part of the woods, caught breathless into that fairy circle like a stolen, enchanted child . . . Loveliness shook her, as a wind shakes a leaf. These strange, dizzy moments lurked hidden in the world like fairies in a wood, and at any hour they sprang forth and seized her, and the emotion, however often repeated, was each time as keen. They would spring forth and grip her, turning the daedal earth to magic, at any lovely hour, in wood or lane or street . . . She was stabbed through and through with a beauty sweet as honey and sharp as a sword, and it was as if her heart must break in her at its turning. After this brief intensity of joy or pain, whichever it was, it was as if something in her actually did break, scattering loose a drift of pent-up words. That was how poems came. After the anguished joy, the breaking loose of the words, then the careful stringing of them together on a chain, the fastidious, conscious arranging. Then the setting them down, and reading them over, and the happy, dizzy (however erroneous) belief that they were good . . . That was how poems came, and that was life at its sharpest, its highest intensity. Afterwards, one sent them to papers, and it was pleasant and gratifying if other people saw them and liked them too. But all that was a side-issue. Vanity is pleasant, gratified ambition is pleasant, earning money is very pleasant, but these are not life at its highest power. You might at once burn every poem you wrote, but you would still have known life.

When Rose was in her late twenties and in her thirties (this was when her early novels were being published) her poetry added up to a couple of slim books, *The Two Blind Countries* and *Three Days*. But after the end of the First World War, when she met Gerald O'Donovan—she was then thirty-seven—it seems that she wrote less and less poetry. In her broadcast 'I speak for myself' she had something to say on this. She described how, as she grew older, the world of 'imagination and fantasy' gradually slipped into the background:

[That] other world went on: it didn't fade away with childhood, or even with adolescence, though . . . my visits to it became less frequent . . . I believe it to be true that you cannot have exciting human relationships at the same time as frequent complete surrender to the dream. Friendships, love affairs, even amusing intercourse, tend to absorb, filling the outer world so successfully that the inner retires. But even then there are moments when it surges up, one falls into it, poetry takes hold, one swims in it as in a sea. It becomes richer, and more mature and less egotistical than the dream world of childhood; adventure and daring deeds give place to the more passive excitement of beauty and strangeness.

Such a moment when it 'surged up' came to Rose in her late forties, when she was just back from a holiday in America with two of her family. Asked to contribute some poems to a new Gollancz anthology, she confessed to Victor Gollancz that 'Starting on poetry is like turning on a tap, with me. The trouble is to turn it off again.' Here it is specially interesting that the two months in America had been two months away from Gerald.

It does seem almost certain that Gerald did *not* encourage her poetic impulse. We know that he did not care for *They Were Defeated*—the book which many people, including Rose herself, thought was her best—in which the youthful heroine suffers so deeply when her lover scorns her poems, refuses even to look at them. But an element of doubt remains as to whether Rose did or did not write poetry during her attachment to Gerald, because when her flat was bombed in 1941, and all her papers and letters were lost, there *may* have been poems among them—we cannot tell.

During her last years Rose again wrote poetry occasionally, and till the end of her life she was sensitive and vulnerable about it. At the start of her correspondence with Father Johnson, when they were getting to know one another, she shyly sent him some of her early verses, and was clearly much disappointed when he failed to grasp their meaning. He asked her to elucidate them, and she wrote back full of apologies: 'Those poems were written at very different times, some when I was quite a young girl . . . All rather fanciful, I suppose. But don't worry about them. Of course I should, and do, write differently now. My outlook is different, as you can imagine. But also I don't write so much poetry as when younger; one doesn't, I think.' This was one of the very few matters in which Rose found Father Johnson lacking in understanding. The subject of her poetry was dropped. But she did not forget her disappointment. Four years later, in 1955, just after the trip to Turkey which inspired *The Towers of Trebizond*, one of her letters to Father Johnson includes this remark: 'I wondered if I should cut out and send you a poem by me in the *Times Lit Sup* last number, but remembered that you don't care for my poetry, so didn't.' The poem in question was entitled 'Dirge for Trebizond', and here are a few of its stanzas:

Where now is Byzantium its lost last empire?
Where the Grand-Comnenus in his palace on the crag?
Their magnificence the emperors, Alexios, Andronicos?
They sat beneath the gold roof set with stars,
The floors were rose marble, the walls bright as flowers.
They were Byzantines, with libraries and such;
They talked of homoousion, babbled of the Trinity,
In the Greek of Trebizond.
Oh the glitter of the churches, chanting their Masses
Within the painted walls, where Christ and his emperors
Stood stiff and bright, like trees!
The library of Tychicus, the marbles, the glory,
The Trebizond princesses, straight as palms,
The rich merchant cargoes, tossing up the Euxine
From the Golden Horn to Trebizond!

In the fig-grown palace ghosts whisper
In the Greek of Trebizond.
Among the broken walls and the brambles
Feet pass round and about:
Trapezuntine shadows, they remember
Five centuries ago.
There is talk of the Trinity, talk that the barbarians
Howl round the walls like the sea:
Mahmud's Janissaries, Mahomet the Sultan:—
Will Eugenios save, or the Gold-Haired Virgin,
From their chapels on the hills?
Kyrie Eleison, Christe Eleison, Kyrie Eleison!
The Emperor David parleys at the gates . . .
The Sultan and his hordes pour through.
The barbarians are in.

. . . So I hear them whisper, the Trapezuntine ghosts,
As they roam the forlorn end of time,
On the Pontic shores, by the bitter lake
Where Ovid cried in vain to Rome;
Where, crying and praying, he came at last to terms
With life and death and Caesar and fate,
And the Pontic shores, and the storm-tossed gulf,
And that dark, that menacing gate.
Domine, Domine exitus mortis:
But there are no exits now.
The last pass sold, the last hold lost,
The citadel stormed, the life-lines broken.
We knew Byzantium once, now no more.

So here we find yet again, in one of Rose's last poems, the
melancholy of the poetry of her youth. And there is also deep

melancholy—as well as tragedy—in *The Towers of Trebizond* itself, though the gaiety and absurdity are more often remembered. In *Trebizond* Rose did indeed reveal her paradoxical self. And perhaps inevitably this has given rise to misconceptions, especially as to her religious position. One can hardly blame those who, lacking an understanding of her special kind of humour, have assumed that the fun she pokes at the Church, and her criticisms of it, indicate that she was at heart an unbeliever. As regards her beliefs she was certainly unorthodox—some would say heretical—and she readily admitted this; but that is a very different thing from absence of faith.

When the letters to Father Johnson were published, they helped to establish the facts, but some of the ideas they left were superficial. If there were ever to be such a reference book as a *Who's Who of Religious Belief* the entry for Rose Macaulay might read something like this: 'Brought up Church of England, suffered doubt in adolescence, took to Anglo-Catholicism in her twenties, lapsed for nearly thirty years, sometimes ridiculed Christianity, eventually returned to the Church, ended her life a happy Anglican.' All true, yes, but a misleading over-simplification. For Rose's faith went very deep. Her heart was involved profoundly, as well as her independent, sceptical mind. It may be that her mind was the mind of a man, but her heart was the heart of a woman. There were times in her life when she smothered and denied her faith, but it was always there. '*Am* I "fundamentally religious", I wonder?' she once wrote to Father Johnson. 'I suppose in one way it would be difficult for any of my family to escape something of this, with our long lines of clerical ancestors on all sides. I think I naturally believe in some kind of mysterious world, interpenetrating this world, in and out of it and all round its margins.'

So *this* was where her religion and her poetry merged! In fact her early poetry may be seen as a foreshadowing of the religious experience that in her last years was to come to its daily eucharistic fulfilment, and to bear its fruit in the transformation of her life, in the qualities of kindness, gentleness, and compassion which those who knew her less well attributed merely to the 'mellowing' of old age. But although Rose was profoundly thankful for her homecoming to Anglican practice, in a spiritual context she did not regard herself as 'having arrived'. Though intellectually she was often as sure of herself— arrogant even—as ever, spiritually she was learning humility.

There is a telling expression of this in the epigraph at the beginning of *The Towers of Trebizond*. Ostensibly taken from a work entitled '*Dialogues of Mortality*', it is in fact Rose's own composition:

'The sheening of that strange bright city on the hill, barred by its high gates . . .'

'Barred from all, Phrastes?'

'From all, Eroton, who do not desire to enter it more strongly than they desire all other cities.'

'Then it is barred indeed, and most men must let it go.'

'Those who have once desired it cannot let it go, for its light flickers always on the roads they tread, to plague them like marsh fires. Even though they flee from it, it may drag them towards it as a magnet draws steel, and, though they may never enter its gates, its light will burn them as with fire, for that is its nature.'

'Who then were the builders of this dangerous city?'

'Gods and men, Eroton; men seeking after gods, and gods who seek after men. Does it not appear to you that such a fabric, part artifact and part deifact, reared out of divine intimations and demands, and out of the mortal longings and imaginings that climb to meet these, must perpetually haunt the minds of men, wielding over them a strange wild power, intermittent indeed, but without end? So, anyhow, it has always proved.'

In Rose's view this epigraph, which she called her foreword, was extremely important. But most of her readers hurried past it to pursue Aunt Dot and Laurie and the camel. 'Many who read the *Towers* did *not* read the Dialogue of Mortality at the beginning of the book', Father Johnson complained to me after Rose's death, 'and so missed the significance of the whole.' Rose herself, when the book was published, wrote to her sister Jean: 'I am *so* glad you like my foreword. I was a little doubtful lest it should seem to give too solemn and religious a touch, but after all that is what . . . *Trebizond* . . . is largely about . . . the struggle of good and evil, its eternal importance, and the power of the Christian Church over the soul, to torment and convert.'

And what of the intellectual side of Rose's religion? Father Johnson once wrote to me:

I think that the Christian Church was the outstanding *interest* of her *whole* life . . . For a number of years she was living outside . . . the Church's life . . . [and] many of her excellent books were written throughout that period. But there is very little internal evidence in those books of her being outside the Christian fold; indeed I cannot think of *any* which did *not* attract me by the very fact that they contained references to the . . . [Christian] religion, *far* more true and *much* more sympathetic than are ordinarily to be found in the writings of most of the best modern novelists.

Interest in the Christian Church: yes, how right he was! It comes out again and again all through Rose's long career as a writer. Here, for example, are views she expressed in 1924, not long after she had lapsed, a moment when one might imagine she would not have wanted to mention religion at all. 'To observers of human nature', she wrote in an article on 'thinking alike upon religion', 'one of the most interesting things about that very interesting business, religion, is its infinite variety of expression. To turn a Quaker into a Catholic, a Catholic into a Protestant, a Theosophist into a Wesleyan . . . what dull, perverted aims are these! To stamp out and flatten all those interesting diversities of temperament which lead men to follow their Gods by different paths (or rather, to address them in different manners, for following is not, as a rule, what we do)—this would be a stupid enterprise indeed, but one, fortunately, impossible of achievement.'

And then, if we return to *Trebizond,* and listen to Rose, in her maturity, speaking through the ruminations of Laurie on the subject of Truth and the Churches, we find that the 'interest' is still there, but it has now developed into something much deeper.

No Church can have more than a very little of the truth. It must be odd to believe, as some people do, that one's Church has all the truth and no errors, for how could this possibly be? Nothing in the world, for instance, could be as true as the Roman Catholic Church thinks it is, and as some Anglicans and Calvinists and Moslems think their Churches are, having the faith once for all delivered to the saints. I suppose this must be comfortable and reassuring. But most of us know that nothing is as true as all that, and that no faith can be delivered once for all without change, for new things are being discovered all the time, and old things dropped, like the whole Bible being true, and we have to grope our way through a mist that keeps being lit by shafts of light, so that exploration tends to be patchy, and we can never sit back and say, we have the Truth, this is it, for discovering the truth, if it ever is discovered, means a long journey through a difficult jungle, with clearings every now and then, and paths that have to be hacked out as one walks, and dark lanterns swinging from the trees, and these lanterns are the light that has lighted every man, which can only come through the dark lanterns of our minds.

Finally, to bring this lecture to a close, and to remind us of Rose as we last knew her, with her energy and zest and her amused twinkle, as well as her love of beauty, here are some excerpts from her account of the last of her travels, the cruise to the Greek Islands and the Black Sea that took her to Trebizond for the second time. She made the trip in August 1958—only two months before her death—when she was seventy-seven, and her non-stop enthusiasm for climbing ruins and swimming are all the more remarkable in view of the fact that she had only just recovered from a fractured thigh.

Like Marco Polo and many more, we took ship from the Venice quays for our eastward voyage. The *Hermes* lay in the docks, looking more commodious than any vessel Marco Polo had. We were some two hundred souls (for souls we become, I believe, when on shipboard). It was like some embarkation in a Poussin picture, where men run about the quays with bales and corded boxes, and eleven thousand virgins arrive on the Zattere to sail into a sunset sky. Down the Adriatic we steamed, bound for Greece, the Golden Horn, the Pontine Sea . . .
On the third day we left the ocean for Delphi, to climb about the sanctuary of Apollo and the theatre . . . Next day we scrambled about the Acropolis and the dear old Parthenon (has it been improved or damaged by all the work done on it down the ages? I myself feel a nostalgia for its mosque and minaret days, but then I have a passion for *mélange* and the fantastically impure) . . .
Next day we abandoned culture and landed on Skyros, our first Greek island, to swim in a sea of translucent rippled jade . . . But we could not linger; we were sailing to Byzantium, which we saw sprawling magnificently over the Golden Horn as we sped into the Black Sea . . . And so to Trebizond. To me it was like coming again into the enchantment of a dream . . . Istanbul was an anticlimax; and not, I think, to be loved. We were glad to leave it for our last Greek islands . . . At Lemnos we spent a morning swimming, and climbing up to the medieval castle . . . Aegina was even more romantic. The temple of Aphaia, that wild nature goddess, stands high on a mountain, lonely and beautiful among pines. We scrambled up to it on foot or donkey, and climbed on to its topmost heights. There can be no temple better situated for demanding energy of its worshippers. Having worshipped there . . . we rode our donkeys down again to plunge into a green, rock-bound sea.
Does travel increase our liking for people? is sometimes asked. Surely it must . . . I returned from this voyage phil-Hellene, phil-Turk, phil-Russian and phil-cruiser. An enchanted voyage. Nothing but Venice could have broken the descent to ordinary life on land; but then Venice is not, of course, ordinary life, nor yet life on land; balanced on those perilous piles, she floats, man's loveliest artefact, an evanescent mirage.

And so we leave Rose Macaulay, the writer who wished she could be remembered as a poet, in Venice, the place which towards the end of her life she loved more than any other. Its magic echoed her happy Italian childhood, and the novel she had just begun—it would have been her twenty-fourth—was to be called *Venice Besieged*. Her life had come full circle.